SADDLE UP
YOUR OWN
WHITE HORSE

SADDLE UP YOUR OWN WHITE HORSE

5 PRINCIPLES EVERY
WOMAN NEEDS TO KNOW

Saundra Pelletier

Tilis Publishers
(866) 688-4547
www.tilispublishers.com

Ordering Information
Quantity sales. Special discounts are available on quantity purchases by corporations, associations, and others. For details, contact the "Special Sales Department" at the number above.

ISBN 978-0-9797961-0-4

Printed in the United States of America
FIRST EDITION
13 12 11 10 09 08   10 9 8 7 6 5 4 3 2 1

This publication is designed to provide accurate and timely information in regard to the subject matter covered. It is sold with the understanding that neither the author nor the publisher is engaged in rendering professional advice or services to the reader. The author and publisher are not associated with any manufacturers of the products mentioned and are not guaranteeing the safety of these products. The author and publisher shall assume neither liability nor responsibility to any person or entity with respect to any damage caused, or alleged to have been caused, directly or indirectly, by information provided in this book. If you do not wish to be bound by the above, you may return the book within thirty days of purchase, together with proof of purchase, to the publisher for a full refund.

To Leta Anderson Pelletier.
If all mothers raised their daughters as
you raised me, there would be no need for
my book. Thank you for making me
believe that I am extraordinary.

CONTENTS

Preface ix

Introduction 1
How to Use This Book

Principle 1
Deliberate Creators Make Their Dreams Happen 11
Victims
Flatliners
Deliberate Creators

Principle 2
Women Possess Two Unique Gifts 39
Multitasking: Our Blessing, Not Our Curse
Intuition: We No Longer Will Get Burned at the Stake

Principle 3
Women Must Lead in Their Relationships 53
with Men
Take the Lead with Your Money
The Best Way to Get a Hero Is to Create One
Adoption at the Altar
The F Word

Principle 4
No Woman Is an Island: Every Woman Must Create
a Cavalry 79
We Women Need to Stick Together
Cavalry Members
How to Hire Members of Your Cavalry
A Cavalry Can Keep Us Healthy

Principle 5
    Women Must Master the Three Cs: Confidence,
    Credit, and Comfort with Success   103
        Competitive Feminism
        What Must Women Learn to Achieve Success?
        The Three Cs

Epilogue: Never Confuse Motion with Action   141
        Change Your Attitude
        Inside Looking Out

Appendix A: Resources   151

Appendix B: Twenty Pregnancy Tips   163

Appendix C: Where to Give Back   171

Notes   175

Index   181

The Author   185

P utting yourself first is the least selfish thing you can do for others because it gives you more to give back. As I think about the experiences that led me to this belief, and to this book, I realize that since childhood I have been groomed by a series of extraordinary women to be an advocate for all the women who need a louder voice, a broader shoulder to lean on, or a squeaky wheel to represent their needs.

I grew up in Caribou, Maine, a small town distinguished only by the fact that it is the northernmost city in the contiguous United States. Women in this farming community were told that they had only two important choices in life: whom they would marry and how many children they would bear. My mother felt oppressed by this mentality, so when I was five years old she told me, "Domestic skills won't get you out of Caribou, so you leave those to me, and I'll teach you what's really important."

Instead of dusting or cooking, my household tasks included balancing the checkbook, educating my younger brother, and organizing all family activities. I was raised to "saddle up my own white horse" instead of waiting for Prince Charming to arrive on his noble steed. After all, I had a lot to accomplish before he arrived.

My mother's reluctance to raise another Betty Crocker became blatantly obvious when I started kindergarten. Everyone else had a regular school lunchbox, but not me. I had to carry a red briefcase because, according to my mother, school was not about *eating*, it was about *progress*. I also had to wear suits, much to my dismay. I often wonder where my mother found those suits in a place like Caribou, but I can assure you that she was quite resourceful.

I cannot remember ever being treated like anything other than an adult by everyone I interacted with—people seemed to follow my mother's lead. My mother discussed everything with me, and I was allowed to present my case for any issue I deemed worth debating. If I had a compelling argument, I could actually win. It was fabulous.

I once made my case to watch *Dragnet* every morning before the school bus arrived. I told my mother that I learned valuable negotiation techniques from the show, so my Pop-Tart and cereal breakfast also included a suspense episode with Sergeant Friday.

Grade school and junior high presented many obstacles of inequality that helped me to understand the fine line between being an advocate for a cause and being a nuisance. When I failed home economics in junior high, I was able to persuade the administration to change the curriculum and got myself enrolled in fly tying and arc welding—two "boys only" classes. (The skills I learned in those two classes have provided me more benefits than sewing and pie baking.)

In high school, one of my favorite teachers was the smartest person I had ever met. She challenged me by introducing me to great literature and encouraged me to allow my outside to reflect my inside and not to follow the pack. She inspired me to speak words that changed the way other people thought. She was also secretly a lesbian, and she hid her sexual orientation as though it were a horrible dirty secret that would get her burned at the stake. In my town that wasn't too far from the truth, so I kept her secret like a clandestine code that existed among a select few.

In my freshman year, I asked her to be my coach when I was an exhibition speaker, which involved presenting meaningful monologues that moved us in some way. My competitors chose to recite presidential inaugural speeches or comedy monologues, but I wanted something shocking. I chose a scene from Lillian Hellman's play *The Children's Hour* that confronted the local townspeople's beliefs and values because of the play's lesbian theme. I used two different voices and two different stances and had a very dramatic death scene on stage. My father almost went into cardiac arrest, and my mother, of course, gave me a standing ovation.

I never felt the need to conform. I always stood up for my beliefs, and it never occurred to me to ignore my intuition because I knew my mother was in my corner cheering me on.

I believe that everything happens for a reason, and though we might not clearly see the reason at the time, the lesson is still learned. Just before my sophomore year, my parents sent me to New York to spend the summer with my fourteen-year-old cousin. My parents pooled their meager finances for the trip because my mother thought that the journey would be a much-needed experience, and my dad thought that being around a "normal" teen would "fix" me.

As it turned out, my cousin and I had nothing in common. Instead, the person I was destined to meet was Shaundra, the girlfriend of an older cousin. She was an actress and the most beautiful woman I had ever known—with all the confidence and flair I imagined a movie star to have. I, on the other hand, was a pudgy mess.

When I told Shaundra that I wished I looked exactly like her, she replied, "Honey, you should look like you, only better. Every woman is beautiful, but she has to feel it or she can never show it." That summer I lost weight, cut my hair, changed the kind of clothes I wore, and started seeing myself differently. Shaundra encouraged me by saying that she would do anything to have my brains because then she would be unstoppable. It was quite a summer.

In college, I was saddened to find out that many women were there to find husbands rather than to improve their minds. It became my mission to encourage the women I met to find themselves first and to believe in their own worth. Through my experiences, I came to believe that the value women place on their partners versus themselves is the fundamental reason so many women find themselves alone, wondering why they can't attract a "good man." They wind up acting too needy or too strong. Neither of these behaviors will get us what we want.

I put myself through school by simultaneously working four jobs—the most interesting was being a DJ for Stephen King's radio station—so I was embracing multitasking to its highest degree. Graduation brought job interviews that I thought were unfair to women. But after I spent several hours being a squeaky wheel, I was allowed to interview with companies outside of my degree expertise.

Although I had my heart set on working in television and becoming the next Connie Chung (she was very popular then), I also interviewed with two pharmaceutical companies. One of the companies had launched the first birth control pill and had a reputation for being a leader in women's health. So when the manager offered me a handsome salary, a company car, and an expense account, I decided it would be a good steppingstone until I "made it" in broadcasting.

Ten years later I was still working in the pharmaceutical industry. I had successfully maneuvered my way up the corporate ladder with eight promotions and five relocations and had developed a reputation for doing whatever it took to succeed. I had more dings in my armor than a knight in battle, but I understood that sometimes you must be willing to pay a price for success.

I had accomplished goals that had largely been considered unattainable. I joke that I had a healthy dose of unconscious incompetence: I didn't know what I didn't know, so I thought I could do anything. I represented a portfolio of women's brands and launched them all over the world. It was my dream job. I took my job very seriously, working six days a week and traveling fifteen days a month, but it was all for women. What could be nobler?

The dream came to an end after my first encounter with competitive feminism—women hindering other women from succeeding. A jealous woman, who felt threatened by my success, became my supervisor and decided to send me out of the country permanently. Rather than fight fire with fire, I decided to let karma take its course. I set my sights higher and moved on to a more lucrative opportunity.

I then went to a company that had an impressive board of directors (including Deepak Chopra) but attempted the impossible— to be all things to all women. We conducted extensive market research on human behavior and the preferences of women. The research solidified everything I thought to be true about the amazing creatures called women, and I feel blessed to be one.

We tried to answer Sigmund Freud's question, "What do women want?" and more importantly, "What are they not getting?" The research concluded that the two top concerns of women everywhere were loss of libido and aging. The reason for this was their uncertainty of how these problems would impact their relationships with their partners.

My "aha moment" came during one of the last peer discussions. A woman stood up and asked, "What are we supposed to do now? What about our dreams and our desires? Most of us have put ourselves second so our children could have a great life and our husbands a robust career and we would do it all over again, but does that mean we have given up our dreams? Are we supposed to forget about what we wanted to be?"

At first these questions made me very sad, and then I became very angry. I was upset that men got to "have it all" while women stood on the sidelines. A very wise woman I knew suggested that before I swore off men, I needed to "fraternize with the enemy and get a male perspective." Since I thought my friend was wiser than I was, I took her advice.

All the men I spoke with shared the same sentiment: they simply wanted their wives to be happy—whatever that meant. They were willing to bend so that their wives didn't resent them. They validated the adage "When momma ain't happy, ain't nobody happy."

So where is the disconnect? Women are raised to be pleasers, mediators, and martyrs. And it is tacitly suggested to us that there is nobility in putting ourselves second. The key lies in our one most critical decision—that of our own self-worth. Will we act like victims or like deliberate creators? The answer will change every chapter in our lives.

All my life experiences were signs that I am supposed to share the truths I learned so you can put yourselves first and feel good about it. My stories are your stories.

My passion is for igniting women to give themselves permission to care about themselves first. We are the complex enigmas that we want men to be. We are extraordinary not only because we can make our own dreams come true, but we can make others' dreams come true too.

Acknowledgments

This book was not a solo effort, of course. I want to thank my husband, Christian, for giving me unlimited support—even in moments of complete insanity but most of all for being my definition of the perfect husband and father. Thanks to my son, Ford, for teaching me that discussing poop can feel more important than winning the lottery.

I also want to say thank-you to my brother, Troy, for being the best person I have ever met and to my dad for always keeping me balanced by showing me a male perspective.

I appreciate Aunt Lu for validating all the confidence my mother instilled in me and for wanting me to leave my hometown for the sake of every woman who was trapped there.

Special thanks go to Aunt Martina for believing in my potential and intervening just in the knick of time.

My gratitude also goes to my best friend, Doranne, for being *every* member of my cavalry, for letting me be every member of hers, and for sharing her fabulous insight on my book title; Chet and Sylvia Naylor for their focused support; David Naylor for helping me share my message; and Susan Naylor for validating that women united can make things happen.

Additional appreciation goes to the Offenbacher sisters, in particular, Mary Roberts, who has held a steadfast vision for the success of this book, and to Bruce Allen, whose friendship always helps me keep my eye on what really matters.

Thanks to Beth Lieberman for her patience, guidance, and belief in me and this project just when I needed it and then some. And last but certainly not least, thanks to Sharon Goldinger, who has staunchly supported this project with passion, a sense of humor, and an iron fist. I am grateful to all.

W hat grade would you give your life? If your life is not at least a B+, it needs to change. Whether you're twenty-two or seventy-two, you can start living deliberately now. Life is a game of inches, and you need to start somewhere. If you change one situation in which you behave as a martyr, you will make monumental progress.

What do I mean by "martyr"? My dictionary defines "martyr" as "one who makes great sacrifices or suffers much in order to further a belief, cause, or principle."[1]

A martyr mentality tricks us women into believing that there is nobility in putting ourselves second. But in fact, the suggestion that we need to put everyone else first is a cruel farce that blinds us to the possibility of "having it all." This archaic idea pigeonholes us into preconceived roles as caregivers, when providing care is merely one aspect of our incredible capabilities. We need courage and strength to live a truly fulfilled life, and being a martyr does not lead to fulfillment.

Following one of my seminars, a thirty-year-old woman named April approached me, looking relieved. She said, "My whole life, I put my brothers and sisters first because I was the oldest child, so I had to help my mother. Now I do the same thing at work, at my church, and in my family—and the only person suffering is me. I have so much resentment, but I keep doing it again and again like I'm an addict. I hang on to the thought that it is my burden to bear and I am comfortable feeling sorry for myself. Today that changes."

It is almost unnatural for us to think about ourselves first. We feel selfish if we take care of the one person who keeps it all together for everyone else. Yet when we are happy, when we are fulfilled, don't we have more to give back to others? Instead of hoarding our joy, we share it. When we shine our brightest light, we are irresistible and our positive outlook is contagious.

A martyr mentality robs us of the opportunity to leave a stamp of authorship on our own lives. All of the significant contributions that we could make above and beyond our day-to-day responsibilities are merely unfulfilled dreams. Consciously and subconsciously, we women are raised to be pleasers who forgo our own desires so our husbands, children, siblings, and coworkers can have more. But just because we can do a lot for them, does that necessarily mean we should? Is having broad shoulders and thick skin our burden to bear forever?

Many times we don't make decisions based on what we want because we have too many other people to consider. Women have been programmed to please and the mental tapes that replay again and again tell us that as soon as we do this "one last thing" for someone else, we will then take time for ourselves. Unfortunately, that time rarely occurs.

Once I coached a woman who had built a reputation as a pillar in her community. Her social club, her church, and her family all knew that if they called upon her, whatever they needed would get done. She had convinced herself that this reputation defined her. She told me that she had always planned on seeing Italy in her retirement. She also wanted to explore the possibility of participating in an archeological dig, and she dreamed of learning the game of tennis well enough to beat her neighbor in a friendly match. However, she told herself that all of these desires were frivolous. In addition, when she shared these desires with her children and her three siblings whom she supported emotionally on a daily basis, they all said that she would have plenty of time for herself when she reached eighty. Her pastor reminded her that the church needed her energy to help build the congregation, and her social club friends said that if she wanted to travel, she could plan the annual group trip to Sonoma so they could all get a vacation. She wanted *me* to give her permission to be selfish—that's how she put it. After a lifetime of service to others, she sat in my office asking a stranger to tell her to value her own worth.

I am proud to tell you that she loved Venice. She also planned a trip for her social club on the plane ride back and was inspired to develop some new fund-raising ideas for her church while enjoying some Italian vino.

Too many women accept as fact that they can quietly enjoy life, but living life to the fullest is something that has been reserved for someone else. We believe that we are supposed to derive our joy from putting ourselves second and knowing that we helped others achieve their dreams. We are trained to accept the idea of sacrifice as though it were our blessing. Women who want more for themselves and actually take it are stereotyped as being "bitches on wheels." And who are the worst culprits? Ourselves. We have chosen to believe the society-imposed nonsense that keeps us down. We have decided that limitless abundance in every aspect of life is not a woman's option.

Do you believe that you can have it all? Why not? Is it because you're too busy meeting everyone else's needs to even consider that you may be sabotaging yourself? Your to-do list, however effective it is for getting things done, will *not* reveal your desires. You need to focus on what you really want. Examine what that is, and then stop making excuses for accepting anything less. This is the best way to accomplish your goals, to fulfill your dreams.

In my seminars, I teach that true balance comes when you actively listen to the wake-up calls you receive and adjust your actions accordingly. Only you can decide what "balance" is and what adjustments to make. I believe that balance includes having the chutzpah to be unpopular—to live by rules that you create and that align with your core values regardless of what other people think, say, or do.

The ability to perceive wake-up calls is tied to your intuition, so tune in and don't live with blinders on. For example, getting sick is a wake-up call that you need to take better care of yourself. Being thrown a curve ball by a family member or an employee is another kind of wake-up call. For example, if your child unexpectedly fails a class or a key person in your division quits, it's a sign that you haven't been paying enough attention to what's happening.

Maybe you're worried that if you embrace your own power you will be considered a feminist. After all, in some circles, "feminist" is a derogatory word. Pat Robertson once said, "Feminism encourages women to leave their husbands, kill their children, practice witchcraft, destroy capitalism and become lesbians."[2] Why would you ever want to embrace that?

I, however, have actually spent my life trying to be categorized as a feminist because I knew that it would mean I was a strong, independent woman who had abandoned her martyr mentality. I have always thought of feminism as a way to defend the unique gifts that come with being born a woman. It seemed to me that any woman who was categorized by the media as a feminist was merely standing up for equality. She was pointing out the elephant in the room and speaking the truth. So I considered feminists crusaders for justice. I also thought that those who opposed these feminists were inflexible bigots, so if I had to choose a side, there wasn't much to think about. Admittedly, as I succeeded in business, I quickly learned that feminists were commonly seen as squeaky wheels, extreme troublemakers to be avoided by anyone climbing the corporate ladder. Unfortunately, this negative sentiment came from both men and women.

As you read this book, I hope you will embrace a new positive term for "feminism": "deliberate creator." Stepping up to be counted and to fulfill our true potential is our main responsibility in life, and women are by nature better equipped than men to make dramatic and purposeful changes. But how many of us command the top spot on our own priority list? Starting today, we need to forcefully say to ourselves, "I am willing to live deliberately and take responsibility for getting what I want."

Perhaps you would like to earn a graduate degree, travel to foreign lands, build your dream house, care for the environment, improve your community, raise dogs, sing, or run a marathon. What's holding you back? Chances are, you tend to ignore your own deepest desires in favor of fulfilling the dreams of those around you. Well, guess what? The time has come to stop using self-sacrifice as an excuse. The first step on the road to a fulfilled life is to clarify what is most important to you. What are your core values? What are your passions?

A critical factor in determining what's important to you is recognizing the distinctions between your dreams and others', whether your partner's, children's, parents', or boss's. Do not substitute someone else's dreams for your own. Compromise is part of all healthy relationships, but creating something that works for everyone means that the concessions aren't entirely yours. Shared lives include shared goals.

This book is meant to be a lighthearted smack in the head to get you to realize that leaving a stamp of authorship on your life is a privilege. Our only responsibility is to show the world who we really are, what we are made of. When we can do that, we will be able to contribute more to others than we could by concealing our true potential. The most heartbreaking, frustrating, and maddening trait women possess is the willingness to set aside (or the inability to even recognize) their own potential and to live an unfulfilled life.

My goal is to make you realize that not only is putting yourself first the least selfish thing you can do for others, but it is also the best way to give back. I designed five principles for empowering women based on five core aspects of every woman's life, including yours:

- ☐ Your attitude toward yourself
- ☐ Your understanding of the innate characteristics and skills inherent to women
- ☐ Your relationships with men
- ☐ Your relationships with other women
- ☐ Your relationship with success, power, and prosperity

The principles provide a map illustrating the shortest distance to personal and professional achievement. They are a result of my own experiences, conversations with empowered women, and exchanges with women who disclosed their disappointments in life. They are practical, common-sense guidelines that will assist you on your life path. Each principle is covered in one chapter of this book.

- ☐ Principle 1: Deliberate creators make their dreams happen. This chapter explains why you need to saddle up your own white horse and put yourself first. It identifies the three choices we have for living our life: to be a victim, a flatliner, or a deliberate creator. The decision you make will determine your regrets or your accomplishments at the end of your days. The attitude required to transition from one choice to another is clearly defined.

□ Principle 2: Women possess two unique gifts. This chapter discusses the appropriate steps and exercises to help you clarify your core values, create a mission statement, and discover what you are naturally good at. It will help you either validate that you are making the right choices or identify new options that you need to explore. You'll discover the value of acknowledging your God-given female traits.

□ Principle 3: Women must lead in their relationships with men. This chapter explores the many roles that men and women play in their personal and professional relationships. It offers skills and techniques for effective communication as well as the secret to a lasting romantic relationship.

□ Principle 4: No woman is an island: every woman must create a cavalry. This chapter explains why you need goddesses, queens, and heroines on your side. Every woman must have a cavalry and also be a member of one to effortlessly get what she needs in life. You will learn the six critical criteria for "hiring" the members of your cavalry.

□ Principle 5: Women must master the three Cs: confidence, credit, and comfort with success. This chapter reveals the five most valuable leadership qualities, the five steps to building confidence, ten presentation tips to show and prove your confidence, three ways to give and receive credit, and seven ways to be comfortable with success in your professional life.

How to Use This Book

You can read this book two different ways. The first way is to simply pick it up and read it from beginning to end. You will find that the information has a natural flow. The second way is to focus on specific areas of need that are impacting your life today. Once you have extracted the helpful hints you need, go back and explore the remaining principles. Each of the principles can stand alone, and all chapters can be treated as reference sections for you to refer back to.

The stories in the book are those of real people, but the names have been changed to protect the innocent—and the not so innocent. The quotes are some of my personal favorites, and they illustrate what I am trying to communicate within each principle. Levity is always helpful as it lends an air of fun when more serious matters are being discussed, so I hope you will find the jokes amusing and poignant. At the back of the book, I have included "A Woman's Declaration" for you to photocopy and sign so you can keep your commitment to change close at hand.

The appendix has three sections that are full of useful information. First, appendix A lists the books and Web sites you need to know about. You'll find information about healthy living, pregnancy and motherhood, staying organized, your career, women's empowerment, and more. Next, appendix B distills the advice from all those boring books about pregnancy and tells you the twenty tips you really need to know. Finally, appendix C lists places where you can give back to others. After all, once you start putting yourself first, you'll have much more to give back. These organizations are all doing important work, and they could use your help.

It is my sincere hope that you will find the time spent reading this book to be valuable. I also hope you will revise your to-do list to include your core values instead of spending all your precious time on menial tasks that can either be completed by a member of your cavalry or put on a condensed task list that you concentrate on only once or twice a week. Revisit your core values regularly to solidify your commitment to achieving your goals and to track your progress. If you've never saddled up a horse, it's time to learn how, and if your horse is already saddled, don't wait around for a knight in shining armor. Go after your dreams.

Deliberate Creators Make Their Dreams Happen

Each one of us has a choice as to how we embrace life. You could choose to be a victim, a flatliner, or a deliberate creator. Which one are you?

1. Do you believe that your life circumstances are beyond your control? Does life just happen and you react to it?
2. Are you a magnet for controlling, self-absorbed individuals?
3. Do you often find yourself agreeing to take on tasks or participate in activities that you really don't want to do?
4. Do you behave as a pleaser so you can avoid feeling guilty about saying no?
5. Do you compare yourself to others who are worse off so you can feel better about yourself and what you have accomplished?
6. Do you approach your job or tasks with the intent of "just getting them done"?
7. Do you believe that successful people were raised with silver spoons in their mouths, married into money, or just got lucky along the way?
8. Do you put the needs of others before your own and feel noble in doing so?

9. Do you set goals for the future that you consistently never meet?
10. Do you voraciously read self-help books, attend seminars, and complete courses and never seem to integrate any of the teachings into your own life?

If you answered yes to any of these ten questions, it is time to begin your transition from victim or flatliner to deliberate creator.

Victims

If you have chosen to be a victim, you allow your energy to get drained by people who are takers. You often rationalize and justify why you tread water. Your favorite expressions go something like this: "I have no choice; bad things always happen to me" or "I made my bed; now I have to lie in it." If a victim has someone else to dote on, such as a child or a lover, she will shower that person with adoration and compassion. If she has no one to care for, she will adopt the "poor me" syndrome of self-pity. She believes that her situation is always someone else's fault. She is never to blame or responsible. When you are a victim, you have low expectations for yourself because you either don't think you deserve better or don't think you're capable of having what others have. You have given up on wanting more and believe that your ability to improve your lot in life is zero.

Chloe is a victim. She has had her heart broken a thousand times, and she will tell you that she can't attract a good man. She claims to have "jerk radar," which attracts men who are trouble. Her parents are divorced, she's been divorced herself, and she subconsciously walks into every relationship with the expectation that it will end. Her mom could never find a good man, and she can't either. She frequents the same places where she meets the same type of man again and again because that's what she's comfortable with. She says that all the other women around her are younger, prettier, and smarter than she is so they attract all the good men. All that remains for her are the leftovers. She behaves desperately and lacks confidence because she's sure that each romance will be temporary. She relives the same relationships over and over again, getting exactly what she expects.

Alisa is another victim. She has been a sales manager for five years. During that time, she has watched three of her colleagues get promoted to positions she wanted. She will tell you that her boss has it in for her. If performance were the deciding factor, she says, she would have been promoted because her team's sales revenues are higher than the revenues of any other team in the company. When I asked her about addressing this issue with her boss, she said it was no use because he wouldn't listen. She believes that's the way it is, and although she wants a promotion, she won't take a step to promote change. Instead, she complains about a situation that only she can control.

Then there's Brinn. Three years ago, her husband cheated with her best friend and left Brinn for "the other woman." Instead of moving on, Brinn has become a man hater, consciously and sub-consciously she is raising her children to blame their father for ruining their lives. She is desperately lonely, drinks too much, and wallows in self-pity. What she doesn't understand is that the best revenge is a new, better life, not a life focused on the past.

Are You a Victim?

If you find yourself thinking or saying the statements below, you are a victim:

- ☐ "There's nothing I can do about it. The decision is already made."
- ☐ "If I had been treated better as a child, I would have more confidence in myself."
- ☐ "Too bad I don't have 'skinny genes.'"
- ☐ "Wealthy people have to step on too many kind people to be successful. At least I can say I never do that. Maybe I won't be rich, but at least I can live with myself."
- ☐ "Even though I know I'm not his priority, it's better than being alone."

Victims waste valuable time thinking about what they don't have and often blame parents, siblings, or others for their perceived misfortunes. We cannot change the past. Do not linger there. We can only change our present, and that will change our future. You are who you decide to be today, at this moment. If you are not happy with any aspect of your life, you can make a deliberate choice to start making changes today. That's the power you have every minute if you only embrace it. Don't be in denial and don't waste time beating yourself up about what you cannot control. Moving forward and embracing a positive attitude toward change is the first step in making change happen.

Flatliners

If you have chosen to be a flatliner, you have accepted a life of plain vanilla. Think of a brain-activity monitor that has gone flat. While the comparison is harsh, it may ring a bell that brings you back to consciousness. When you're a flatliner, you decide that "settling" is a worthy state of being: you have accomplished just enough in life so coasting through your remaining years is acceptable. Your entire life is predefined. You know all the outcomes because you make the minimal effort to get the same recurring results.

**If we don't change, we don't grow. If we don't grow,
we are not really living.**

Gail Sheehy

You expend your energy on completing to-do lists, but your tasks are not aligned with your core values. Because you get a lot done, you convince yourself that you have made progress. But you simply relive the same day over and over again, like Bill Murray's character in the movie *Groundhog Day*. You justify your state by saying that your life is good enough. It's better than most others' lives—better than your parents' lives were, better than your brother's or sister's life, and better than the lives of the people in your immediate circle. Wanting more is gluttonous; it's greedy. No one promised you a rose garden, you tell yourself and those who care about you. "It is what it is," you say. "Real life is not like the movies" and "I should be grateful for what I do have."

A flatliner focuses on her immediate situation, often using her spouse and children as excuses for not taking action: "My kids come first, so going back to school is selfish. I'll do it once they leave home." She thinks it's more honorable to make choices that benefit others instead of herself.

My hometown of Caribou, Maine, was full of flatliners. When I was growing up, Saturday was "women-and-children" day. While the other kids played outside, I would stay inside to play cards for money with my mom and her friends. The game, Scat (usually played for nickels and dimes), was really just an excuse for the ladies to vent, get advice, and make plans to kill their husbands. No murders actually occurred, of course, but my education in the secret thoughts of women started early. These women held nothing back on my account, and by the age of twelve, I had heard enough about the real feelings of women to last a lifetime.

These flatliners, who had all settled for "good enough," had a bond in misery. They had more than their mothers had and so, they reasoned, they should be grateful. They felt the world ended at the county line. Wanting more would fall into the realm of fantasy, so why bother? Their advice to me focused on how I should pick a husband because that act had defined their own lives. Even though these women loved each other, they didn't want any member of the group to have a better life than their own. They didn't want to hear success stories about other women because that wasn't what bonded them. The consensus in the group was that most of the success stories were made up anyway.

You don't have to be a small-town housewife to be a flatliner. Beth has practiced law for fifteen years while raising three children. She has watched nine of her peers (eight men and one childless woman) become partners while she has been consistently overlooked, even though her track record of wins for litigation is 95 percent—second in the firm. She knows exactly why she's been passed over: The problem is that she goes home to her husband and children at five o'clock instead of schmoozing with her co-workers after hours. Although she will tell you that she makes great money, has a nice office, and doesn't need to become a partner to be happy, her tone and body language give her frustration away. She will also tell you that her situation is fair because she gets to spend all the time she wants with her family, takes a vacation every year, and doesn't take work home every weekend. What she *doesn't* say is that the partners also take time for their families, don't take work home, and enjoy annual vacations. Beth seems to ignore those facts because accepting less is easier than fighting for what she really wants.

Heidi is another flatliner. Her intuition told her that monogamy was not Jeff's strong suit but he was the man she had been looking for all her life. They have been together four years, and though they care deeply about each other, their relationship has developed into one based on a brotherly/sisterly kind of affection. She is a comfortable security blanket that he can come home to after his wild trysts on business trips. Although they never discuss his infidelity, an undercurrent of tension is always present. She believes that he will eventually change his ways and convinces herself that what they have is better than what most people have, so she should be grateful for a kind, supportive partner who simply has one flaw. Her father was a wonderful man in most respects, but he was unfaithful to her mother on and off throughout their fifty-year marriage. For Heidi, infidelity seems to be a comfortable compromise that women should be willing to accept.

Rose Marie always boasts about her youthful days when she had a fabulous figure and was a motorcycle model for Harley-Davidson. She recounts great stories of exciting photo shoots and adoring men who begged for even a moment of her attention. However, the five-foot-five-inch, two-hundred-pound body she has now makes it difficult for others to imagine her younger, slighter frame. Her conversations always end with a comment that now she is really focused on weight loss. She promises that we will see amazing results within six months, but she never keeps that promise. As she ages, her health is deteriorating and carrying this extra weight is obviously a risk factor. However, she views any attempt at intervention as a negative judgment and a lack of acceptance, so after years of nudging, her friends have finally given up.

Are You a Flatliner?

It's easy to recognize complacency in others. But can you spot this tendency in yourself? Here are some examples of flatliners' statements:

- ☐ "I don't need to impress anyone. My life is good enough. Besides, nobody likes overachievers."
- ☐ "I know that a lot of people are worse off than me, so I should be happy with what I have."
- ☐ "Most people who have a lot were born rich, cheated their way to the top, or married into money."
- ☐ "I don't need to strive for more because within my circle of friends, I have the most."
- ☐ "I gave birth to two kids and work a full-time job. I don't have time to look like a supermodel."

Have you been true to yourself? Have you remembered to do what is important to you, what is in keeping with your self-integrity? Although creating a life that works for everyone might be the ultimate goal, women too often ignore their own deepest desires and focus instead on fulfilling the dreams of those around them. So many women conveniently use men and children as their excuse for becoming and staying flatliners.

> **We must overcome the notion that we must be regular. It robs us of the chance to be extraordinary and leads us to the mediocre.**
>
> *Uta Hagen*

Deliberate Creators

Katie Couric is the first woman in the history of television to anchor a national evening news broadcast. She impressed us, charmed us and won our hearts and minds as we watched her public climb to the top of the corporate ladder. I can remember feeling her pain in the days when she politely and diplomatically shared the spotlight with Bryant Gumbel on the *Today* show. His inflexibility often created obvious tension with guests and certainly with viewers like me. Katie stayed focused on the big picture and persevered to become the leading host on *Today*. Yet this was not her pinnacle. As a deliberate creator, she continues to accept new opportunities and to change the way people think.

Billie Jean Moffitt, better known as Billie Jean King, changed the lives of women worldwide when she changed the way we thought of women in sports. She was considered by many to be the outstanding female athlete of the world in 1967 and in 1972 was named *Sports Illustrated*'s Sportsperson of the Year. As a result of her focused efforts to infiltrate a male-dominated sport, she established the first successful women's professional tennis tour. As a deliberate creator, she understood that we live in an abundant universe and what you give comes back to you. Therefore, she founded tennis clinics for underprivileged children.

Suze Orman has earned respect as a financial advisor, writer, and television personality. From humble beginnings working as a waitress, she has successfully maneuvered past the corporate ladder to achieve a reputation admired equally by men and women. Although she has received many professional accolades, she magnified her status as a deliberate creator by honoring the totality of her life and announcing that she is gay. She exemplifies perseverance and has shown that anything is possible if you believe in your ability to accomplish it.

Madeleine Albright was the first woman to become U.S. secretary of state. She has been a consistent spokesperson for women's rights and the importance of women helping other women. She stands as a model of a respected and balanced leader. Her commanding presence never makes us question her qualifications or the fact that she is a woman succeeding in a male-dominated arena. As a deliberate creator, she has publicly admitted her regrets, shown humility, and most importantly, flexed her muscles when appropriate.

Tina Turner is the best living example of a woman who has transitioned from a victim to a deliberate creator. Overcoming severe domestic violence has been one of her many accomplishments. She has been nominated for twenty Grammy Awards and has won eight. She has a star on the Hollywood Walk of Fame and has been inducted into the Rock and Roll Hall of Fame. VH1 ranks Tina Turner at number two on its list of the greatest singers in rock, and *Rolling Stone* ranks her sixty-first on its list of the one hundred greatest artists of all time. Her inner strength and faith in her own ability to reach her goals have prompted a genuine admiration from anyone hearing her name.

Unlike victims and flatliners, deliberate creators live according to a set of rules that they alone determine. They are unconcerned about keeping up with the Joneses. After all, what would the Joneses know about their happiness? Deliberate creators ignore naysayers and are confident in their decisions. They can "agree to disagree" with those who judge or reject their chosen life path. Deliberate creators have well-defined core values, and they will not compromise their self-integrity. They don't have to be leaders of groups or organizations, but they always make sure that any activity they direct their energy toward is aligned with their own mission statement.

Deliberate creators have a solid handle on their emotions and their emotional intelligence. They exert positive pressure to get what they want, and when they encounter obstacles, they find ways around them. They understand that what they focus on will come to them. They are intentional in their thoughts and actions and continually focus on the best outcome for the group as a whole, whether that group includes a partner, a family, a company, or a community. They have a strategic view of the world and their surroundings and a big-picture perspective.

They direct their energy toward endeavors that matter to them, regardless of whether or not they matter to others. Is this behavior considered "bitchy"? If so, sign me up. Deliberate creators' philosophy is "Someone has to be first, so why shouldn't it be me?" If you are a deliberate creator, one of your favorite sayings might be "I will do whatever it takes to make it happen" or "If someone else can do it, I can do it too." Deliberate creators practice *possibility* thinking ("If this way doesn't work, let's try a different way"), *optimism* ("We have all the right ingredients, so the outcome will be great"), and *self-acceptance* ("I'm learning," rather than "I'm no good at it").

Universal Laws of Nature

Deliberate creators understand that successfully reaching their goals can be as simple as following the universal laws of nature, which have been provided in numerous teachings over the millennia. Many people have used various versions of these laws.[1] I have compiled the very best laws that pertain to deliberate creators and have changed some of the definitions so their true meaning is more apparent and applicable to living a fulfilled life. Once embraced, the following laws will ease your transition into becoming a deliberate creator.

Law of Three. The Law of Three says, "*Thoughts* put into *words* create our *actions*."

If a person desires a new home, dreaming of the home and describing it will not magically bring the home to fruition. Dreaming (thoughts) and describing (words) are two steps in the process, but the third and most important step is the action step: actually drawing up the architectural plans and building the home will make it a reality.

Just thinking and talking about what we want will never make it happen. We need to make some deliberate step to show the universe that we are willing to participate in the creative process. Deliberate creators think about what they want, talk about their strategy for acquiring it, and take the necessary steps to make it happen.

Law of the Word. The Law of the Word is "Every word has a positive or a negative charge associated with its meaning."

Choosing positive words in all of our communications will result in positive experiences. Intimidating, manipulative, and judgmental phrases create negative experiences. People often will remember one obscure negative comment that scarred them in childhood ("You'll never amount to anything") rather than numerous positive and complimentary words ("You are so smart" and "You can accomplish anything"). They will either fail or succeed as a result of those words. Deliberate creators choose their words thoughtfully. They get results by understanding the power that a slight emphasis or intonation on just the right word can have.

The real art of conversation is not only to say the right thing in the right place, but to leave unsaid the wrong thing at that tempting moment.

Dorothy Nevell

Law of Correspondence. The Law of Correspondence is "Our outer world is a reflection of our inner world."

Our outer circumstances will be dictated by the inner harmony (or disharmony) we have created in our lives. We are misguided if we think that improving our physical environment will be enough to make us happy. Money by itself doesn't equate to happiness. "More" is not always better. We have bigger houses but broken homes, more medicine but less health, and more technology but less real communication. Deliberate creators realize that success is an internal process.

Law of Compensation. The Law of Compensation is "For everything we do in life, there will be an equal and opposite reaction." Another way to express this law is with the old saying "What goes around comes around." For example, a boss who treats his subordinates harshly will probably find himself being treated that same way by his own boss. Deliberate creators choose their actions carefully and anticipate what reactions they will create.

Law of Surrender. The Law of Surrender is "When we have done everything we can to achieve a goal, turn the situation over to something greater."

We experience a quiet satisfaction when we know that we have done everything in our power to realize our goals. In other words, we have covered all of our bases. We have crossed our *T*s and dotted our *I*s. No stone has been left unturned. Confidence is part of the mental makeup of deliberate creators, and they know that once they have taken all the necessary steps, there is nothing more they need to do. They have faith and know their goals will materialize.

Law of Love. The Law of Love is "In loving someone, we make a full commitment to the total development of the full potential of the other."

Most parents have dreams and desires for their children. We all want our children's lives to be better than our own. Committing to the total development of another human being means having the willingness to relinquish our ideas about what we may feel is best for that person. Sometimes the best lessons in life are the hardest ones to learn, and we simply need someone to unconditionally love and support us through a phase of self-exploration. Deliberate creators know that in order to love others, we need to love ourselves first. Then, and only then, can we truly commit to someone else's full development.

How many natural laws can you recognize in the following story?

> After seventeen years of marriage, a man dumped his wife for his young secretary. His new girlfriend demanded that she wanted to live in the couple's multimillion-dollar home, and since the man's lawyers were a little better, he prevailed.
>
> He gave his now ex-wife just three days to move out. She spent the first day packing her belongings into boxes, crates, and suitcases.
>
> On the second day, she had the movers come and collect her things.
>
> On the third day, she sat down for the last time at their beautiful dining room table by candlelight, put on

some soft background music, and feasted on a pound of shrimp, a jar of caviar, and a bottle of Chardonnay. When she had finished, she went into each and every room and deposited a few half-eaten shrimp shells, dipped in caviar, into the hollow of the curtain rods. She then cleaned up the kitchen and left.

When the husband returned with his new girlfriend, all was bliss for the first few days. Then slowly, the house began to smell. They tried everything; cleaning and mopping and airing the place out. Vents were checked for dead rodents, and carpets were steam cleaned. Air fresheners were hung everywhere.

Exterminators were brought in to set off gas canisters, during which they had to move out for a few days, and in the end they even paid to replace the expensive wool carpeting.

Nothing worked. People stopped coming over to visit. Repairmen refused to work in the house. The maid quit.

Finally, they could not take the stench any longer and decided to move.

A month later, even though they had cut their price in half, they could not find a buyer for their stinky house. Word got out, and eventually, even the local Realtors refused to return their calls.

Finally, they had to borrow a huge sum of money from the bank to purchase a new place.

The ex-wife called the man and asked how things were going. He told her the saga of the rotting house. She listened politely and said that she missed her old home terribly and would be willing to reduce her divorce settlement in exchange for getting the house back.

Knowing his ex-wife had no idea how bad the smell was, he agreed on a price that was about one-tenth of what the house had been worth, but only if she were to sign the papers that very day. She agreed, and within the hour, his lawyers delivered the paperwork.

A week later, the man and his new girlfriend stood smirking as they watched the moving company pack everything to take to their new home—including the curtain rods.[2]

How Can You Become a Deliberate Creator?

To be a deliberate creator, you must first believe it's possible. Your attitude toward "possibility thinking" will have the strongest impact on your ability to change. When you hear "Be careful what you wish for," take heed. What are your thoughts toward what you deserve and what you will settle for? Focus on what you do want, and think about what it will be like to have it. Thomas Willhite wrote "You can have anything in this life you want" if you follow these five simple steps:[3]

1. State specifically what you want. For instance, if you are trying to lose weight, say "I want to lose fifteen pounds by July 15," rather than "I want to lose weight."
2. Want it so badly that it becomes a consuming desire. For example, every morning, read your goal, which you have printed out and taped to your alarm clock, rather than simply randomly thinking about losing weight throughout the day.
3. Have faith in your ability to achieve your goal. Regardless of your previous success or failure at losing weight, repeatedly tell yourself "This time is different" versus "I'll do the best I can."

4. Be persistent in your efforts. Commit to exercising four specific days and times a week rather than fitting exercise into your schedule if time permits.

5. Be willing to pay the price for success, whatever that price may be. Giving up girls' night out, happy hour, and Bloody Marys on Sundays is a required sacrifice to achieve your goals. Conversely, a "starve and reward" mentality sabotages your efforts.

Here are some other qualities shared by deliberate creators:

☐ They believe that they need to always strive to do their best. Their success doesn't hinder anyone else from achieving his or her goals because when they raise their own bar, others will strive to go higher.

☐ They want to "pay it forward." They help, encourage, and give generously to others because they believe that they live in an abundant universe and what goes around comes around.

☐ They believe that knowledge is irreplaceable. They realize that being curious and open to new ideas will increase their self-worth.

☐ They tolerate what they cannot control. They understand that 10 percent of life is what happens to them and 90 percent of life is how they react to it.

☐ They practice high intention, low attachment. Once they have taken deliberate and purposeful steps to achieve their goals, they have faith that the desired outcomes will happen. They believe that they can attract the right people and circumstances if they do the right things. They believe that the laws of nature tell us that we reap what we sow, so thoughtful planning, hard work, tenacious drive, and an attitude of prosperity will be rewarded.

Deliberate Creators in Action

Cathy is a deliberate creator. Business had plateaued at her cafe and her profits weren't as high as she wanted them to be. Her partner, being conservative, thought they should just keep doing what they had always done—no more, no less. But Cathy refused to settle for mediocrity. She developed a growth plan that she was certain would work. She believed the restaurant fulfilled an unmet need. When a competitor came to town, Cathy's business started declining even more. Her partner was willing to accept failure and start layoffs. Cathy went to the bank, took out a loan, bought out her partner, expanded the restaurant's physical space, and offered dinner on Friday and Saturday nights. Profits doubled in six months. Why? Because she set her intention and followed through.

Anxiety exists within all of us. It is normal to feel fear when we are embarking on new endeavors, but the difference between being a victim and being a deliberate creator is knowing that opportunity lies in calculated risks.

Brenda left a lucrative position in corporate America to be a stay-at-home mom, a decision for which she made no excuses. When her daughter was eighteen months old, Brenda longed for something more. Everyone had complimented her on how beautiful her nursery was—simply perfect in every way. So she found a marketing guru who was also a mother and offered her a trade: free babysitting in exchange for a Web site, flyers, business cards, and a logo for her new enterprise, NeverLand Nurseries. Brenda has matched her corporate salary in two and a half years' time and is wildly happy because she has the best of both worlds.

Unlike Brenda, most women don't acknowledge or take credit for what they are naturally good at. Defining our mission statement and our core values is nothing more and nothing less than defining what makes us happy and recognizing what comes naturally to us. It is our responsibility to determine what makes us truly unique as individuals and then maximize our God-given skills. That is what makes life worth living.

Deliberate creators know their own worth and will not let anyone devalue them. Diane had spent six years building her corporate reputation, exceeding expectations, and making every right move to get to the top. She worked twelve- to fifteen-hour days, including weekends, and did everything required to get the nod for chief operating officer. When the critical time came, she was passed over for a less experienced peer who had established himself in the "good ol' boys" network of weekend golf and family outings. His wife had helped him seal the deal by joining the right tennis club and attending ladies' luncheon groups. Diane used her diplomacy skills to graciously congratulate the winner and behaved as if it were business as usual. However, three months later she resigned, accepting the position of president at a competitive company.

> **Deliberate creators know their own worth and will not let anyone devalue them.**

Deliberate creators are not always decisive. They honor their self-integrity and follow any path that they genuinely believe will lead to their goals. Some of us know that a focused effort will deliver the desired results; others know that this is an abundant universe and exploration is required. The tie that binds all deliberate creators is having a plan, whether it's focused or experimental. Both approaches are their attempts to reach a desired goal. Consequently, whichever path they choose inevitably leads them to prosperity.

Leslie hadn't chosen a major for college because so many subjects interested her. Most of her friends had selected what their parents had pressured them into. Leslie wanted to have choices. She had a deliberate intention to approach college as an investigative mission to find out what really sparked her interest. Anyone who spoke with her quickly realized that she was not a fickle young lady but a multitalented one. She had a part-time job as a bartender, did work-study for the college newspaper, joined the debate team, and took general education classes as well as electives in astronomy and marine biology. Her studies concluded with a degree in journalism, and today she is getting ready to launch her own magazine.

> **Character cannot be developed in ease and quiet. Only through experiences of trial and suffering can the soul be strengthened, ambition inspired, and success achieved.**
>
> *Helen Keller*

When something is very important to a deliberate creator, the end will justify the means. In 1998, I was in Japan leading a very capable team in launching a campaign for oral contraceptives. The United States had released the first birth control pill (Enovid) in 1960, but the Japanese government avoided this form of liberation for women for almost forty years. The excuses given were absurd and confusing: Estrogens would be released into the environment and contaminate the air. The pill would make Japanese women promiscuous.

We could not convince our Japanese partners that these excuses were unreasonable, so we fought a fight we *could* win. We designed a campaign for men, emphasizing that the pill would be liberating for them and would create spontaneity in their sex lives. The pill would allow men to have mistresses and concubines without the worry of unwanted pregnancy. The campaign worked. As a result, Japanese women now have better contraceptive choices and the freedom to make those choices.

Let me share another personal story with you. I faced a dilemma while I was writing this book. My very calm, predictable husband told me that he wanted to leave everything behind, sell all of our belongings, and go sailing for two years. At first I laughed and thought he couldn't be serious, but I was sorely mistaken. Initially I wondered if he wanted to go alone, but that was not the case. He wanted me to adopt his dream and make it my own.

Stepping out of the daily grind did hold a certain appeal, but I have never been much of a sailor. The idea seemed kind of crazy to me. My husband explained that not only did his mother go sailing with his father for two years, but she took two children—him and his brother.

After much thought, I decided that I couldn't be the person who squashed someone's dream. How could I live with that? Shouldn't I admire him for pursuing his dream with vigor? So I enrolled in a sailing class, and we began to look for a boat. We put our house on the market, sold our cars, and finally bought a sailboat. Everyone complimented me with great enthusiasm for supporting my husband's dream and for having such an adventurous spirit. I thought it was more like temporary insanity, but I accepted the praise.

By now you probably know that I am no prima donna who has been surrounded by luxury. I began picking potatoes when I was six and driving trucks in the fields when I was thirteen. But living on a boat takes a certain kind of person. And that person was not me. Finally, I hit the wall and experienced a case of WIIFM: What's in it for me? Why do I have to uproot my life for someone else's dream? Where's my backbone? What about *my* dreams? I was forced to face my true fear, which was not about sailing or fulfilling my dreams. It was much larger. Maybe I was not matched with the right partner. Maybe he needed someone who was better equipped to handle such adventure. When I told my husband what I was feeling, he "fell on his sword" and said that the sailing trip would be permanently postponed if we couldn't be together.

We eventually agreed on a compromise. Initially we would move to the marina for three months during the summer and rent out our house. I would also get a fabulous new business office in which to write and see clients because I had to leave my home office. This was something I had wanted for months. To everyone's shock, but especially mine, I love living on the water and on a boat. I cannot describe the freedom.

As I was preparing our house to be rented, I was amazed at all the stuff I had accumulated that I simply didn't need and how focused I could be on what I do need. Today we have plans to sail away on an extended cruise when our son is three, and my husband is satisfied at the moment. The compromise is win-win.

Being a deliberate creator means winning the battle for balance by refusing to accept less than you should. It's having the courage to make your ideas known, even when your views are minority opinions. One of the first steps you can take is to set boundaries for yourself and others. Practice saying no. Then learn to ask for help when you need it. Approach every day with the intention of making a little progress toward becoming a deliberate creator. Remember, every journey begins with a single step. Don't judge yourself on where you are today. Accept your situation and commit to changing for the better.

> **Don't judge yourself on where you are today. Accept your situation and commit to changing for the better.**

Kendra had been in a relationship with the same man for five years. On her thirty-fifth birthday, after several margaritas, she decided it was finally time to accept the fact that Cal was never going to be the man standing beside her at the altar. Although they were engaged, he would never agree to set a date. His theory was, if it wasn't broken, why fix it? He recited discouraging growing divorce statistics, described the misery his friends had experienced after marriage, and proclaimed how proud he was for defying society's imposed traditions. Nonetheless, Kendra's biological clock was ticking, and she wanted to be married before procreating. As she explained these feelings to Cal, she could sense his resistance increase. She knew that presenting an ultimatum to set a date wasn't the way she wanted to enter into a lifelong partnership, so she quietly and confidently found another place to live, gracefully packed her bags, and with a hopeful heart, began her search for real commitment.

Deliberate creators believe that prosperity is theirs for the taking. Their achievements inspire others to reach higher, and they attract like-minded people.

Simone had worked in corporate America for eleven years. When she left college, she got her first job and stayed there. She had received six promotions and consistent pay raises. She was on track to be a vice president within two years—that is, until she got pregnant. Her pregnancy seemed to be professional suicide. All the important projects were given to others because she would soon be going on maternity leave and the whispers said that she probably wouldn't be back. *Hurt*, *offended*, and *angry* didn't even begin to describe how Simone felt. She knew her life would change when she became a mother, but she didn't intend for motherhood to be the death of her professional dreams.

In June, Simone's baby was born. During her twelve-week maternity leave, no one from her office contacted her, so she used this time to research all the companies that she would want to work for. She interviewed with several of them. She told the interviewers that she wanted to work only twenty-five hours a week but guaranteed that her work would be equivalent to that of most of their fifty-hour-a-week employees. She received two offers and chose the more lucrative one.

The people in her company were shocked when they learned she was resigning to work for another company. In her exit interview, she said that being pregnant made her feel alienated, discriminated against, and devalued. Today she is the president of the company she joined four years ago, which, by the way, now has an on-site day care center, flexible employee hours, and high employee productivity.

Michelle and Steven had good jobs and made good money, but their dreams were very distant visions because the high local cost of living robbed them of any discretionary funds and their house was on such a small lot that they didn't have room to really breathe. She wanted to plant an organic garden, visit a weekend farmers' market, and have an acre of land. He wanted to build a wooden boat, spend weekends away from work, and enjoy the peace of mind of knowing all their money wasn't going to a tract home on a highway in California. They both were tired of keeping up with the Joneses and felt their children needed a change. They knew their current friends wouldn't visit them in rural suburbia and certainly wouldn't understand their decision, but whose life was it? They packed up the family and moved to South Carolina. They knew no one there, but Steven had secured a job beforehand, and Michelle arranged to work for her current company from her home office. They bought a house they love and are very happy with their choice.

Denial is for victims and flatliners. For example, in Michelle and Steven's case, denial would have kept them in an unhappy life, pretending it was good enough. Deliberate creators take the one life they are given and they live it, as difficult and as complicated as that is to do. They admit their mistakes and make changes with an eye on the future because they know that living is growing, and growing pains happen at every age and at every stage of life.

What Deliberate Creators Know

Deliberate creators know the following truths.

Nothing Has Meaning until You Give It Meaning. Nothing in your life should have more meaning than your self-worth. Each one of us is priceless. Do not let every bad event in your life decrease your opinion of your own value. When events put a ding in our armor, we tend to make a withdrawal from our "self-worth account" instead of making a deposit. Why should our account grow? Because we learned from our mistake and it made us stronger.

This theory is very important to embrace, especially when you're facing a major obstacle as I did the summer of my sophomore year in college. I was working as a disc jockey for Stephen King's radio station, WZON. (The decor was morbid, the music was rock-'n'-roll, and my alias was "Sandy Nelson.") On my mother's birthday, I left work early to make the three-hour drive to Caribou from Bangor. I came upon a blind spot in the road just as a truck was backing into a driveway. It completely blocked both lanes and left me no room to maneuver. I had only a second to react. I grabbed the steering wheel and turned it as sharply as I could. During the car's three complete rolls, I was thrown thirty feet through the air into the woods. I'm lucky I was ejected because the car's roof was crushed down to the driver's seat. As you can imagine, the damage to my body was extensive. My mother was told that my neck was broken and that paralysis was likely.

Once I left the hospital, a very long and arduous recovery was planned for me, including almost two years of physical therapy, lots of medication, and many ruined plans. But instead of just accepting everything I heard, I made a deliberate choice to let my body tell me how fast I could recover. I was committed to getting better as fast as possible, so everything I did was focused on getting better and every day I did a little more. Adhering to someone else's time frame wasn't an option for me. I gave *my* plan more importance than I gave the doctors' plan. I was realistic but optimistic. As a result, I went back to school four months later. I had to make a few adjustments, of course, but my life and schedule were back on track. I gave appropriate meaning to the words and diagnosis each physician provided. Most of the doctors' opinions were speculative, so the determination of success or failure was left to me. They all predicted a long, difficult recovery process and went out of their way to give me permission to wallow in my own self-pity.

No one knows better than you what you can do. Don't accept anyone's opinion of what you can achieve; make up your own mind. Accumulate advice from a variety of experts, but first and foremost, listen to yourself and trust your inner guidance. Whether you think you can or think you can't, you're right either way.

Respect Is Earned. You need to first earn your own respect before you can earn respect from others. You need to honor your self-integrity. Find out what you're good at and ignore what everyone else thinks you should do. You know best what comes naturally to you, what excites you, what you look forward to. Stand up for what you love and decide where you can make a difference. By honoring your own interests, you will automatically be following your joyful inclinations and thus valuing your true creative nature. This behavior is a shining example for all the people you encounter, and they will respect you and want to emulate your actions.

Seek advice only from people who walk their talk. This is particularly critical when selecting a coach, a doctor, or a caregiver for your children. Use your instincts. My pet peeve is people who provide coaching on how to deal with situations they know nothing about. Why would anyone take business advice from someone who has never run a successful business or take relationship advice from someone who is single or three times divorced? Conduct the appropriate due diligence because this is time well spent. Don't let smoke and mirrors direct your thinking. Someone with a fabulous vocabulary is not necessarily an admirable person.

If you need or want help, you will attract people who can provide it. Be inquisitive, compare, and don't underestimate a true connection. Be aware that in some situations, what *usually* works for you won't apply. For example, I normally want matter-of-fact, no-nonsense physicians—the more direct and blunt the better. But when I got pregnant, that standard no longer worked for me. I suddenly wanted and needed a different style of doctor, so I honored that need.

Sometimes a small change makes a big difference, and sometimes a very big change is needed. Always go after what you need. Accept that you're taking care of yourself and that doing so will build your self-respect and gain the respect of others.

Prosperity Is More Than a Thick Wallet. We can be prosperous in every aspect of our life: health, relationships, family, spirituality, career. Nothing has to suffer for something else to prevail. Abundance is truly the best gift of life.

Successful Communication Is the Responsibility of the Communicator. Actions may not speak louder than words if we choose the right words in the first place. When someone doesn't understand the message we're trying to convey, we need to consider that our vague or unclear communication is to blame. We are creating the misunderstanding ourselves.

Deliberate creators adapt their communication style to the recipient's so their words and body language are easily understood. They are chameleons and will even go so far as to use a communication style that's uncomfortable to clarify and solidify an important point. The result is a desired outcome. If having everything we want were like an easy Sunday afternoon stroll in the park, we could all be deliberate creators. In truth, the painful and exhilarating roller coaster of success is what attracts deliberate creators and keeps them wanting more.

Do you still have excuses for not living your dreams? If we really analyzed our motivation and put it in the simplest terms, we would see that we operate from one of two emotions: love or fear. Allowing fear to paralyze our potential and accepting an average, ho-hum life is negating our entire purpose on this planet. Operating from self-love is the natural instinct of deliberate creators and naturally creates the life they want and deserve.

> **Quit hanging on to the handrails . . . Let go. Surrender. Go for the ride of your life. Do it every day.**
>
> *Melody Beattie*

Women Possess Two Unique Gifts

You're standing at your kitchen counter eating the leftovers from your children's plates. As you stare at your reflection in the kitchen window, all you see is a growing to-do list that will never get completed. You wonder how it is that your husband has the luxury of sitting in his favorite chair watching television, and you ask yourself, "Is this what I signed up for?"

You might be tempted to blame your husband for this situation, but men are not the ones who oppress us. We oppress ourselves because we decide what kind of life we are going to live. If people treat us the way we allow ourselves to be treated, who do we have to blame? Can we save us from ourselves? The answer is a resounding *yes*.

Randi continually complained that her husband had the life of a prince. She often jokingly called herself Cinderella because his only responsibilities were to bring home the bacon and interact with the kids one hour a day at dinner. She had a full-time job as a vice president, took care of all the domestic tasks, and volunteered in the community to maintain the family's well-to-do status. After harboring resentment toward her husband for two years, she finally imploded, stating that she would rather be single than married with an absentee husband and father. To her shock, her husband said that she was living the exact life she had created. He had always been willing to do significantly more around the house but why should he volunteer and ruin her self-imposed quest to become a "wonder woman"? After three therapy sessions, she discarded her martyr mentality and split the household chores with her husband. She now calls herself the queen of her castle.

No one is better equipped to be flexible and adaptable to sudden change than women. We can adjust our plans at the drop of a hat and refocus our attention toward something new at any given moment. Our resilient nature allows us to slow down or speed up our pace, depending on the demands of the situation. Unfortunately, however, we tend to adjust our schedules to accommodate everyone else's priorities and needs while neglecting our own. Every moment we manage to squeeze out for ourselves is seen as a victory. We push ourselves hard to fulfill work and family commitments with gusto, yet we allow the commitments we make to ourselves to fall by the wayside. Too often, this cycle continues without our ever taking the time to step back and reflect on what we really want.

You may be thinking that a life of serving others is an honorable life, so I will challenge you to read on. What should take priority is building our own character, supporting our own needs, and becoming the kind of individual others want to emulate. Servitude is something that comes more naturally to women than to men because of our nurturing and mothering qualities. However, a fulfilled life is one in which we embrace the courage to serve ourselves first and believe that charity starts at home.

Woman must come of age by herself. She must find her true center alone.

Anne Morrow Lindbergh

Multitasking: Our Blessing, Not Our Curse

Let's face it ladies, most women can multitask and most men cannot. Once we embrace this simple truth, we can all get on with managing our expectations appropriately. Men have a single-minded focus and can accomplish one task at a time and usually accomplish it well, but multitasking is not their strong suit. Fortunately, behind every great man is a great woman who helps him accomplish more by using her multitasking skills. A man will reach his full potential if he is matched with the right woman, personally or professionally. The key words are "the right woman." Consequently, if a man is matched with the wrong woman, his life will resemble a torture chamber.

Women, on the other hand, can do five tasks simultaneously and not only complete them all on time but exceed expectations. Our ability to multitask is our blessing, our advantage, and our edge. We need to honor this gift and use it to its full potential.

At this point, you need to ask yourself, who will help *you* reach *your* full potential? That answer is simple: ourselves and other women. Men should not be saddled with the responsibility of delivering happiness to women. It is not their responsibility. Their single-minded focus and need to assume the role of "protector" makes them a wonderful foundation, but we must be responsible for saddling up our own white horse in order to be truly happy.

> **Our ability to multitask is our blessing, our advantage, and our edge.**

Our ability to successfully multitask allows us to get what we want. Mastering a variety of competencies is a positive result of multitasking. The more we tackle all the things that need to be done to accomplish our goals, the better we get at doing them. Being able to focus on many activities and people simultaneously increases our ability to achieve results quickly.

However, complications arise when our multitasking activities do not align with our core values. Admittedly, we are all capable of doing ten things at once with ease. But will those ten things bring us lasting joy and satisfaction?

The following analogy is a clear illustration of how we need to prioritize our lives. Imagine that you place six rocks in a jar. These rocks represent the six fundamental parts of your life—yourself, your significant other, your children, your immediate family, your health, and your higher power (however you define that). Is the jar full? No—there's still lots of space. Now you pour hundreds of pebbles into the jar. These represent your job, your car, your exercise routine, your hobbies, and other important aspects of your life. Again you look to see if the jar is full and it isn't. Now you fill the rest of the jar with sand, which flows into the crevices between the rocks and pebbles. The sand represents the mundane everyday tasks that take so much of your time and deserve so little energy— dry cleaning, oil changes, grocery shopping, home maintenance, laundry. The list goes on and on. If you were to reverse the order and put the sand in the jar first, there would be little room left for the things that really matter. In other words, women's curse is not multitasking but the inability to *prioritize* what really matters.

Every day, women make decisions ranging from mundane to major. We make the healthcare decisions for ourselves and our husbands, children, and parents and even sometimes our husbands' parents. We determine where we will get married, live, and send our children to school; whom we will socialize with; what we will eat; and where and when we will vacation. You might be surprised to learn that your choices are really not choices at all. They are simply tasks that keep you running on the hamster wheel of life, depleting your energy so you get stuck in the life of a flatliner. Your time and energy are resources, like the money in your checking account. You must choose how you want them to be spent. If an endless to-do list rules your every action, you are continuously making withdrawals and no deposits. No matter how much you get done in a day, you won't be satisfied because these menial tasks do not align with your core values.

Your Core Values

What are your core values? How can you identify them?

1. Reflect back on your life. Identify your happiest memories and most fulfilling experiences and write them down. Start with your junior high or middle school years and then move on to high school and college. Also think back to the early years of your marriage, motherhood, a new job, life in your first apartment or home, a relocation, a vacation.

2. What do these happy memories have in common? In my own life, some of my happiest moments involved encouraging my schoolmates to recognize their own talents and spurring them on to accomplish more than they thought they could. I was elated when a shy and self-effacing friend suddenly became aware of a hidden talent and brought it forth to shine.

3. Jot down words that come to your mind as a result of these memories. These words will express your core values. Some of the words that came to my mind when I thought of one of my friends acknowledging his or her gifts included "satisfaction," "pride," "self-assurance," and "confidence."

4. Ask yourself this question: are my core values incorporated into my daily life at the present time? If the answer is yes, put

down this book and go out and celebrate because you are among the 10 percent of people who know and understand what their core values are. If the answer is no, take these steps to align your life with your core values:

- Identify the people, causes, and things in your life that are energizing.
- Identify the people, causes, and things in your life that are draining.
- Begin to minimize the time you spend with any activity or people that drain your spirit, and spend more time with people, causes, and things that are uplifting.

Your Mission Statement

A mission statement can also help you identify how to use your multitasking ability. A mission statement is simply a written intention or a goal you want to achieve. It should be no more than a sentence long and easy to recite from memory. For example, my mission statement is "to ignite and empower women of all ages, experiences, and backgrounds to give themselves permission to put themselves first and believe that saddling up their own white horse is not only possible but required."

Identifying a mission statement involves three steps:

1. Choose two or three action verbs that exemplify what you are here to give. Think about what you are passionate about, what you are naturally good at. For instance, I love to speak, coach, motivate, and support. Incorporate any aspect of your life that you want to do more of, whether it's volunteering, teaching, exercising, or dancing. Remember to be absolutely true to what matters most when assessing your happiness.

2. Determine what you stand for. This is where your core values will be incorporated. For example, do you stand for empowerment, freedom, equality, or healing? I stand for creating permission.

3. Decide who or what is the object of your affection. It can be a group of people, a cause, or a particular area of interest. Perhaps you're drawn toward animal rights, the environment, or AIDS research. My personal focus is women of all ages, ethnicities, and backgrounds.

Don't Neglect the Two Essentials

The two essentials on every woman's to-do list are exercise and hobbies. We have to stop viewing these as luxuries that can be enjoyed by men only. Every man I speak to encourages the woman in his life to take time for herself, yet the martyr in us tells us that we simply have too much to do. Don't automatically turn your nose up at the suggestion of "indulging" in exercise and hobbies. Exercise is one of the best tools we can use to take care of ourselves so we can operate efficiently. Physical activity relates directly to self-esteem because we feel confident when we look and feel good. Our self-worth increases when we acknowledge that we are honoring our bodies, and we feel powerful when we can do more because we have more energy.

Examine how much time you take for yourself. Your exercise routine can be as simple as taking a thirty-minute walk three times a week (but it should be *at least* three times a week). In the spirit of true multitasking, you can combine your exercise with your hobby and kill two birds with one stone.

Caroline is an example of a woman who combined exercise with a hobby and realized unexpected benefits. Following menopause,

Caroline was unhappy with her new pudgy appearance. She committed to both a fitness routine and increased social interaction to force herself out of her introverted comfort zone. The one thing she knew for certain was that she loved the water. It provided a serenity that seemed to distract her from her daily pressures. To her surprise, she found herself at an Introduction to Surfing Divas course. At fifty-six, she was certainly the most "tenured" student in the course. Her natural charisma made her very popular with her fellow students, as well as with several promoters for the women's surfing circuit. Now, two years later, she has the body of a thirty-five-year-old and the confidence of a nude model. In addition, she is a successful motivational speaker, encouraging "midlife women" to embrace their personal and physical power.

Combining a hobby with exercise isn't the only way to multitask. Many hobbies can be turned into home businesses. A dear friend of mine has become a certified wine connoisseur via mail and the Internet. She began by ordering video lessons and various wines. Then she took an online course one night a week for fourteen weeks. She now conducts home parties for women and gets paid to teach them that they can drink great wine on a beer budget. Her business is called Classy Wino.

Intuition: We No Longer Will Get Burned at the Stake

Women ignore another key characteristic that sets us apart from men because we confuse instinct with intuition. Instinct is what *looks* good, *feels* good, *tastes* good, *sounds* good, and *smells* good (using our senses). The part of the brain that controls instinct is twice as large in men as in women—hence their desire for so much sex. Intuition is the silent dialogue that exists within us, helping us determine good from bad, right from wrong.

Not only do women feel emotion more intensely than men, but we can intuit emotions in others and therefore have more impact than men on the outcome of any situation—if we listen to our intuition. Let us not forget, women were burned at the stake in Salem for simply using their intuition. No wonder we have ignored this extraordinary ability for so long.

In *The Female Brain*, author Louann Brizendine confirms that a woman's intuition is based upon fact. According to Brizendine, "Women have 11 percent more neurons than men in the part of the brain that controls memory and emotion." Our communication center is bigger, so we notice more, feel more, and have more impact when we speak. In other words, when it comes to brains, we are the "superior sex." The problem is, we have been convinced that we are merely equal.[1] Brizendine asks some pertinent questions about a hypothetical comparison between two brains and comes to a novel conclusion:

> What if the communication center is bigger in one brain than the other?
>
> What if the emotional memory center is bigger in one brain than the other?
>
> What if one brain develops a greater ability to read cues in people than another?
>
> In this case, you would have a person whose reality dictated that communication, connection, emotional sensitivity, and responsiveness were the primary values. This person would prize these qualities above all others, and be baffled by another person with a brain that didn't grasp the importance of these qualities. In essence, you would have a female brain.[2]

Unfortunately, instead of relying on our intuition, we have been trained to use "tried and true" methods and to rely on conventional wisdom for guidance. Many men have created pathways to success using such techniques, so we think we should emulate them. We find a myriad of excuses and logical reasons why we should not follow our women's intuition, but these are all mistakes. Imagine hearing that men had a special, unique, and powerful gift that they chose to ignore because society had deemed it a farce. Wouldn't women encourage men to ignore society's misguided ideas and to use their talent?

> **God gave women intuition and femininity. Used properly, the combination easily jumbles the brain of any man I've ever met.**
>
> *Farrah Fawcett*

Here's my theory about why women don't use their intuition. Early in history, a few smart men were intimidated by the fact that women could easily and effortlessly run the world if they wanted to. So the men developed a strategy to convince women that the best use of their abilities was to spend all of their time caring for and nurturing their men and their children. And we believed them! You may have heard the saying that the smartest thing the devil ever did was convince us that he didn't exist, and this applies to a woman's intuition as well. We have been sold a bill of goods. It is time to regroup and treat our intuition as a muscle that becomes stronger with use.

Remember, intuition is the silent dialogue that occurs only within women. It is our responsibility not only to listen but also to keep using this compass to guide us to what is right and away from what is wrong.

How can we maximize the use of our intuition? Start by trusting it and then acting on it immediately. However, always use diplomacy. You will be amazed at how great you will feel when you follow your intuition and how you can subtly and very effectively change the outcome of situations. For example, I once suspected that a friend's husband was cheating on her. I had no proof, but all the signs pointed to infidelity. Rather than destroying my friend's trust by making bold, unfounded accusations against her husband, I suggested that she surprise him with visits at his workplace, the golf course, and the gym, just to show him she cared. To her dismay, he was "MIA" at two of the three scheduled outings at which she showed up. This was the impetus she needed to raise her own suspicions and help her move from a place of denial to an acceptance of reality so she could move on with her life.

Here's another way I used my intuition. I have an acquaintance who, three years after giving birth to a daughter, was still carrying thirty-five pounds of pregnancy weight. She despised that her husband kept bringing up the fact that she was overweight, even though he couched his nudging by saying that he just wanted her to be healthy. Some of her friends had enabled her to be self-destructive by encouraging her to eat and drink whatever she wanted, yet I knew her marriage was suffering as a result of her stubborn mind-set. I casually asked her, "Wouldn't it make you feel great to wear your prebaby jeans again, and shouldn't you be more concerned about how you look and feel rather than what your husband thinks?" She has thanked me five times since that conversation for stating a simple truth in a gentle fashion.

Sometimes using your intuition can rescue you from a difficult situation. For example, at the end of a series of important interviews, Laurie sensed that she had misstepped with one interviewer. Even though the conversation had been professional and polite, she knew she had miscommunicated a few of her points and that her mistakes would hurt her chances of getting a job offer. She e-mailed everyone a thank-you note that night and took special care to connect with the one person she was uncertain about. In her message, she stated how much she had enjoyed meeting him. Then she wrote that she wanted to fully clarify her answers because she felt she may have misrepresented her true meaning. When she was asked back for a second interview, that person saw her in the lobby and thanked her for her e-mail. He said it had really made a difference in his opinion of her. Using her intuition turned a negative into a positive.

> **Never let something go that you can easily fix. You will always feel good about changing what you can control.**

Never let something go that you can easily fix. You will always feel good about changing what you can control.

Using your intuition can be the element that ensures smooth outcomes in professional and social interactions. Women know how to say the right thing at the right time and what to leave unsaid. We do the "little things": we remember birthdays, the names of other people's children, and someone's favorite food or movie, and we acknowledge these with genuine interest. We ask the right questions because they come naturally to us. We can get away with schmoozing or even "brownnosing" because it looks like normal conversation due to our feminine touch. On the other hand, when men schmooze it is often seen as a self-serving effort to get what they want. Women need to use their natural gift of building rapport more often and not reserve it for just our immediate family and friends. For example, Anita's very picky boss happened to mention that his all-time favorite childhood movie was *Chitty Chitty Bang Bang*. This conversation took place months before his birthday, over cocktails at a national meeting when a trivia game was being discussed. When his birthday arrived, the entire staff chipped in for dinner and basketball tickets. Anita contributed to the group gift, but she also placed on his desk a wrapped copy of *Chitty Chitty Bang Bang* with a picture of the movie cast. This thoughtful gesture set her apart from the crowd.

To make the most of your intuition, always write down the critical little details about other people—their spouse's, children's, and pets' names and their birthdays, hobbies, or favorite cities—because you need them in your arsenal. You can make others feel special by doing something special for them. One of the greatest human fears is the fear of being insignificant. Everyone wants to be memorable, and when you remember specific information about others, you will make yourself special to them.

Some time ago, I learned that my boss's wife loved antique teapots. When I went to an estate sale in Maine, I happened to find a beautiful teapot that I was able to purchase for a minimal price. I knew that she was the person who bought my Christmas and birthday presents, even though it was my boss who handed them to me. So I wrapped the teapot and asked my boss to please give it to his wife. I enclosed a card thanking her for always making me feel special. That gift was an important step in setting myself apart. This type of personal gesture is especially important in your professional world if you are single because it is important for your boss's wife to believe you are an asset to the company, not a detriment to her marriage.

Emotional intelligence is another form of intuition, and it is really a woman's trump card. Character is an old-fashioned word for the body of skills that emotional intelligence represents. "Character," writes Amitai Etzioni, the George Washington University social theorist, "is the psychological muscle that moral conduct requires."[3]

Women can sense when a hidden obstacle is delaying progress. This ability is a monumental advantage in the workplace. Men tend to bulldoze through issues to check them off a list, and this prevents them from achieving maximum results. Women naturally want a win-win result. They have the emotional intelligence to acknowledge the "elephant in the room" and say, "It seems like this isn't resonating with you. Are we on different pages? Let's work this out so we can both feel good about it." Open statements like this about an obvious disconnect build more loyalty and camaraderie than you can imagine.

Women's intuition tells us when to intervene, but working in male-dominated companies sometimes stops us from acting on our insights. Too many women ignore their natural sense of perception because they see men operate without it and believe that imitating men will produce successful results for them as well. In fact, the opposite is true. Reading the signs that are transparent to us allows us to leverage situations and get results that are new and better.

Intuition also allows us to deliver tough messages with professional grace and diplomacy because we can read others and understand how to best adapt our communication style to mitigate a bad outcome. Diplomacy is an undervalued skill that gives women an advantage in navigating the steps of the corporate ladder. It allows us to be judicious with strong opinions and find ways to massage unpopular beliefs. (If you're the mother of a teenager, you're likely to have a leg up in this area because you've already had to hone this skill.)

We will no longer get burned at the stake for using our unique gifts, so instead of hiding them or downplaying their significance, we must recognize and nurture our multitasking abilities and our intuition, knowing they serve us well.

Women Must Lead in Their Relationships with Men

In order to create positive outcomes, we women need to subtly take the lead in all our relationships with men. Every honest man in a successful female-male relationship will admit that his partner calls the shots and it's okay with him. He'll say with a laugh, "She's the boss. Just ask her—she'll tell you."

FOR SALE BY OWNER
Complete set of *Encyclopedia Britannica*, 45 volumes.
Excellent condition. $1,000 or best offer.
No longer needed, got married last month.
Wife knows everything.[1]

As we discussed earlier, the Law of Love involves making a commitment to the total development of the full potential of another person. Women naturally practice this law with the men in their lives. Yet too often we do not expect our commitment to be reciprocated.

The essential qualities of love are appreciation, respect, and understanding. We need to evaluate all of our relationships and determine whether they meet these standards. Only when they do will we receive what we truly deserve. Too many times we fall prey to age-old excuses that allow us to remain in inadequate partnerships. For example, we tell ourselves that the other people are too stressed to reciprocate our attention and genuine concern. We silently congratulate ourselves for being strong and acknowledge that we can forge on without support. However, this behavior does not honor our self-integrity; it masks our needs and builds resentment.

It's time to stop putting others' wishes before your own. Ask for what you need, and accept responsibility for communicating your desires to others. First and foremost, creating fulfilling relationships means looking yourself in the eye and telling yourself that people treat you the way you allow yourself to be treated. This may be a difficult step to take, especially if you have chosen the role of victim. Victims find it easy to blame others for their inability to change their situation. But you need to realize that simply talking about the life you want isn't going to make it happen. To get better results, you need to make better decisions and take action on them.

Many of us stay in unfulfilling relationships because if we actually do complain to our partners about the lack of support we receive, they remind us that they are not mind readers and place the blame back on us. We accept the blame and although a temporary change may ensue, eventually our partners' old habits return and we find ourselves as disenchanted as we were at the beginning of this vicious cycle. Don't let silence be your enemy. Make your desires known and don't settle for less than you deserve.

> **Nobody can make you feel inferior without your permission.**
>
> *Eleanor Roosevelt*

We women have the ability to control the success or failure of all our relationships, and our talent to adjust and be flexible is what affords us this power. If we choose to adapt and make the appropriate adjustments needed, the relationship will succeed. If, however, we are unwilling to move, the relationship will end. The decision is ours to make.

Think about this. If we deem a situation unacceptable, we will not allow it to continue. Conversely, if we think it is salvageable, we may make ourselves very uncomfortable to see it through. Women will go to dramatic lengths to pursue a romantic "light at the end of the tunnel." However, wise women know that men follow our lead, so if we feel strongly enough about the potential in a relationship, we can make the appropriate changes needed to make that relationship work.

Male-female compatibility is not a matter of "us versus them." The simple truth is that we want men in our lives because they offer us a solid foundation, a grounded, rooted rock on which to build. Men are our maximum attraction, our perfect complement. We like to have and sometimes need a masculine perspective so we can step away from our natural emotional reactions and responses. When someone upsets us, other women will console us. Men, on the other hand, will tell us why the other person was wrong and that the person's reaction wasn't about us but about his or her inadequacies or ignorance. Problems arise when women expect a man to bridge the gap between them and happiness. However, if we are unable to take responsibility for our own happiness, then we will also be unable to attract the kind of mate that we fantasize about.

> **We women have the ability to control the success or failure of all our relationships, and our talent to adjust and be flexible is what affords us this power.**

Take the Lead with Your Money

Too often, women postpone serious life decisions, using the excuse that once they are married, their choices will change. They delay buying a house, making investments, and planning a financially secure future because they think these are decisions that need to be done in collaboration with a mate. This is a mistake. According to a Hewitt Associates study, women save less than men for retirement. Many households led by women live under federal poverty levels, and many female baby boomers are headed for a rough ride in retirement.[2] When women bank on the words "till death do us part," they are often left with an empty savings account and nothing but debt to base their financial future on because the man in the partnership exits this world well before his life insurance policy has the chance to kick in.

When I met Calle she was thirty-two years old. She had two roommates, five maxed-out credit cards, and no money in the bank, and she lived from paycheck to paycheck. She was smart and talented yet fixated on the idea that once she met the right man and got married, she would get pregnant and stop working anyway, so why bother climbing the corporate ladder or getting her finances in order? Besides, she reasoned, she needed to spend money on going to nightclubs and buying $400 handbags, cute outfits and several cosmetic touch-ups in order to attract Mr. Wonderful. Her entire focus was on finding a man to complete her.

Five years after I met her, she became my client. Her sessions dealt with her resentment about raising a daughter alone, working a full-time job that she was overqualified for, and begging her "evil ex" to spend time with his child. As Calle's example shows, we cannot predict the future, and leaving our financial future in the hands of anyone else is irresponsible.

It is our responsibility—not only to ourselves but to our children if we choose to have them—to be our own breadwinner. That is the best way to attract the kind of man who will be able to support us to our deathbed. The difference is between *choosing* to be financially supported and *needing* to be. Need shifts power and control away from us and eliminates our choices. And when that happens, we find ourselves accepting less than we deserve because we feel trapped. Our self-respect erodes when we operate from a position of desperation instead of one of control.

Fortunately, we have many ways to build and maintain our self-respect. One crucial way is to maintain control over our own money. In any successful partnership, joint financial contributions are important but not more important than individual independence. In January 2007, Oprah Winfrey had a program on money matters. One guest explained how she was left with nothing after a divorce. She said that if she had to do it over again, she would have contributed to a savings account in her own name. Winfrey agreed, saying "I think that's the new feminism, to have a savings account in your own name."[3]

Why would a woman consider any other option? A joint account is a great way to save for a family vacation or build a college fund, but adult independence requires that we control our own checking and savings accounts. After all, my husband doesn't need to know that I bought a $200 pair of boots. By the same token, it's okay for him to buy a $300 fishing pole without telling me. (Sometimes ignorance really is bliss.)

In a partnership, the most effective financial arrangement is based on a fair determination of each person's contributions. A partner who makes significantly more money needs to make a significantly higher financial contribution to the family as a whole. However, if a woman is a stay-at-home mom, her contribution should be rewarded equitably. Forgoing an outside income to raise the next generation has an immeasurable price tag.

The woman of the house needs to have a separate account that she can use as she deems appropriate. Some of my clients find this suggestion absurd. What I find absurd is relegating 100 percent financial control to one individual in a relationship that is called a "partnership." Perhaps the definition of "couple" needs to be changed. Currently the dictionary definition is "two persons considered as joined together, as a married or engaged pair, lovers, or dance partners."[4] Here's a better definition: "two separate individuals who come together by choice while keeping their grown-up independence and separate checking and savings accounts."

Most men are not raised to be as loyal to women as women are to men. No songs are entitled "Stand by Your Woman." A man may be loyal to his mother and his best friend but not necessarily to his woman. On the other hand, if a man supported a woman while she went to medical school or if he worked all hours of the day and night and sacrificed everything for a woman's career, she would be loyal to him until the day she died (or until the day he did, anyway).

What creates this disconnect? Most men think their first responsibility is to be as happy as possible, which sometimes makes loyalty play second fiddle. Accept this fact of life. If you can't support yourself and you think a man will be your breadwinner for a lifetime, you'd better have at least one of two circumstances in your favor: you share a primary residence in a community property state or you have rich parents.

I am most frustrated when I see a woman stripped of her financial security after a divorce. Women are raised to be pleasers and told that our most critical value is in childbearing and child rearing, and we are judged if we choose to work after giving birth. So many of us stay at home and raise our kids, but then our spouse finds us uninteresting and leaves us for another woman.

We are then supposed to just pick up the pieces, find a job, and move on.

To avoid finding ourselves in such a situation, we need to create our own safety net. Be loyal to yourself first, which includes having a backup plan: an education you can fall back on, a skill you can refine while taking care of your kids, an online course you can complete during nap time. Choose something that will help you support yourself financially—and will make you more interesting at the same time.

Trophy Wife

Men are now much more agreeable to having an independent woman as a wife. In fact, "trophy wife" has a new definition. According to Deborah Siegel, today's men are less interested in the "arm candy" factor. Instead, high-achieving alpha women are highly sought-after partners. In a Match.com poll, about half of the men reported dating women who earned the same income as they did. "Old school" thought would have us believe that men choose women based upon their appearance and disposition alone. But today's men are redefining the ideal wife and actually feel relieved when they meet their financial equal. As Siegel writes, "Men in their 20s and 30s embarking on first marriages are relieved to no longer be the sole breadwinner and decision-maker, a burden many watched their fathers shoulder."[5]

Some confusion has arisen because several reports have concluded that men may be more intimidated by high-powered women than they're willing to admit. They secretly feel these women will outgrow them or have unrealistic demands as to what they should contribute and deliver as "the man of the house."[6]

Nando Pelusi, a New York City psychologist who specializes in alpha-alpha pairings, shares this wisdom: "Being involved [with high-powered] women is like driving a Ferrari. It can be uncomfortable and dangerous, but it's ultimately more rewarding than owing a Ford Taurus, which is safe but boring."[7]

Atlanta psychiatrist Frank Pittman says, "Older men want the most impressive achiever in the office. In the eyes of a man's peers, the woman with the career and degrees count for more than Miss America. Status is attached to a woman who is successful, not to a woman with a perfectly pear-shaped ass."[8]

I've noticed that the most attractive men are attracted to women who have a "life plan." A man really wants a woman who could have it all without him but chooses him nonetheless. This fact is the secret to finding the "good" man that all women are seeking. You need to be worthy of a "grade A" seal yourself to be selected by a "grade A" mate.

Jack was going to be married to Jill, so his father sat him down for a little fireside chat.

"Jack, let me tell you something. On my wedding night in our honeymoon suite, I took off my pants and handed them to your mother and said, 'Here, try these on.'

"So she did and said, 'These are too big. I can't wear them.'

"So I replied, 'Exactly. I wear the pants in this family and always will.' Ever since that night we have never had any problems." Jack thought that might be a good thing to try. So on his honeymoon, he took off his pants and said to Jill, "Here, try these on."

She did and said, "These are too large. They don't fit me."

So Jack said, "Exactly. I wear the pants in this family and I always will, and I don't want you to ever forget that."

Then Jill removed her pants, handed them to Jack, and said, "Here, you try on mine."

He tried and said, "I can't get into your pants."

So she said, "Exactly. And if you don't change your attitude, you never will."[9]

The Best Way to Get a Hero Is to Create One

In the best male-female relationships, the women develop their heroes. This may take a lot of work, but it's well worth the effort in the end. Think about this logically. When you invest in your job, you get more rewards. When you invest in your health, you look and feel better. So when you invest in refining your partner, you have lasting happiness. Praise goes a long way with men. Nagging and complaining are like treading water—you move a little, but you don't make much forward progress. Focus on what *is* working in your relationship instead of what is *not* working. The most effective way to get action from a man in any situation is to create the idea that only he can handle it. He is the hero who can save the day. When you praise women, they wonder what you want, but when you praise men, they want more of it, as long as the praise seems genuine.

> Focus on what *is* working in your relationship instead of what is *not* working.

Darcy took my advice and started praising her husband's good behavior. At the time, he was disconnected from their kids because he felt that it was the mother's role to help with the homework and interact with the kids on weeknights while he unwound with a glass of Cabernet. When he did spend time with the kids, Darcy complimented his technique and talked about how much they admired him and the positive ways that he impacted them. This did increase his interaction, but she wanted to know this behavior would continue. An excellent way to ensure good habits is to praise men not only privately but publicly. I told Darcy to begin having phone conversations within earshot of her husband in which she told friends and family how lucky she felt that Tom was such an influential role model to their kids and how much progress they made when he had time to share his way of doing things. It was that easy. He told Darcy that he wanted to help with the homework at least two days a week, and although his schedule might change sometimes, it was important that he spend more time with the kids.

If you need a favor from your spouse or significant other, patting and caressing him is a very effective technique. Always thank him by saying "What would I do without you?" If you can get away with it, actually say, "You're my hero" or "You are a prince" or "I just adore you." And of course, sex will almost always solidify the deal.

Let's not forget to also focus on refining ourselves. Even though we are almost perfect, we need to always lead by example when it comes to change. For example, if you expect your man to be nicer to your friends, demonstrate that behavior with his friends. If you would like an afternoon to yourself, suggest that he hang out with his friends while you do the same. If he needs to improve his eating habits or weight, do the same yourself, even if you already practice good habits. Most importantly, change some pet peeve that he has about you.

If you need a man to take action in a professional relationship, you can use one of two tactics. If you are the man's boss or a peer, tell him, "Things just get done better when you step in" or "The way you do things always gets results." If you are the man's subordinate, let him know how much you admire him: "I learn so much from you and wanted to ask how you would handle this particular situation." If the action needed is one that someone of his authority level must initiate, say, "I know you would want to know about this situation because you have such high standards. I want to provide solutions, so I have thought of some alternatives."

In professional settings, men love to receive acknowledgment and accolades. They want to know that they are completing their duties effectively while developing the admiration and appreciation of others. Keep in mind that compliments from women at the office have a different meaning and magnitude than compliments from women in a social setting. Many men perceive that we are not as threatening professionally as we are personally. They see women in professional settings as team members and support staff—members of the crew helping them steer the "big ship"—so use that perception to your advantage. Most men secretly think they are superstars professionally, so your endorsement only validates their thoughts. A few kind, genuine remarks made in private will shift a man's focus toward helping you reach your goals. His innate "fixer" wants to accomplish the tasks at hand and move on, and if he is helping a "damsel in distress," that's even better.

Never think of men as the enemy in work settings. Instead, think of how you can recruit them to your side to support your agenda. There are too many of them, so we can't beat them; therefore, we need to join them on their playing field and adapt their rules of engagement to meet our needs. Large meetings are usually not the most effective forum in which to get our points heard. Having side conversations, making time for private one-on-one meetings, and forming alliances is the best strategy to lead in professional relationships with men. Gain their support privately and then maximize it publicly. We need to stop playing nice and start playing smart.

> **Because I am a woman, I must make unusual efforts to succeed. If I fail, no one will say, "She doesn't have what it takes." They will say, "Women don't have what it takes."**
>
> *Clare Boothe Luce*

In a marriage partnership, as in any partnership, both parties want something. It's the proverbial WIIFM: What's in it for me? When you develop a plan that makes sure both parties' needs are met, everyone will be satisfied.

For most women, sex plays a prominent role in our lives whether we like and want it or not, and men are always ready and willing to have it, regardless of any "family strain." It seems that sex supersedes relationship issues for men, and most men believe that as long as they are having sex with their partner, their relationship isn't broken. However, it's hard to feel desire toward a man who makes very little contribution to the home besides a paycheck or for a man who doesn't honor and value what you do as a wife or mother. But your man will never know this unless you tell him. Remember, however, that nagging him to help more around the house is not an effective form of talking. It may be quick and easy to do, but it is a waste of time: either the message gets blocked out or a task gets done *only* when you nag. Assertive women understand that a subtle approach is the most effective way to change a man's habits. You must always catch him doing something *right* and overfocus on that action. Too often, we focus first on what is not working. This merely solidifies a man's belief that our expectations are unrealistic.

Keep in mind that people change over time. If we believe that we are constantly growing, then we must accept that we are constantly changing. The woman and man that you and your partner were when you started dating may not be the people you are today. Certainly your needs are different now than they were ten years ago.

In every stage of our life with a partner, we need to lead by example to make sure our needs will be met. If we want a surprise birthday celebration, for example, we need to plan a surprise for our mate first. For my husband's birthday I hired a "romance concierge," which is much like a travel agent but instead is a "love agent." Like a good travel agent, the romance concierge makes the plans and you simply have to show up.

A limo picked up my husband and me and took us to our first stop: a gondola ride with champagne and chocolate-covered strawberries. This was followed by dinner at his favorite restaurant, where he was served his favorite meal accompanied by his favorite red wine. We were then escorted to a decadent dessert restaurant for, yes, his favorite dessert. The evening ended with his getting an autographed T-shirt from his favorite basketball player and, of course, sex.

On a subsequent birthday, I bought him two Lakers tickets and had arranged for his best friend to join him for the big event. Honestly, it was like a "get out of jail free" card for me. Although I happen to like the Lakers, I definitely preferred that his best friend take "my" seat, and I knew my husband secretly preferred it too.

Because both of these birthday events were unexpected and surprise occurrences, my husband could not fall into his typical birthday routine: "What do you want for your birthday? Tell me what it is and I'll buy it." This year I got a surprise spa day with my best friend, including a mimosa breakfast and a wine lunch. It was fabulous.

The purpose of my story is to encourage you to set up your mate for success, not failure. If a man knows what to do, he will do it almost 100 percent of the time. Remember, a man can never have *women's* intuition. To tell the truth, you could meet a woman today for the first time, and in three months she would select a more personal and coveted birthday gift for you than your husband of ten years could. Accept this fact; don't try to change it. Simply communicate with the man in your life so he can meet your expectations. If you are unwilling to take this advice because it is *unromantic*, you will be disappointed.

Men are not mind readers, so make your expectations known or you may find yourself in a situation like the couple below.

> While attending a Marriage Encounter Weekend, Walter and his wife, Ann, listened to the instructor declare, "It is essential that husbands and wives know the things that are important to each other."
>
> He then addressed the men: "Can you name and describe your wife's favorite flower?"
>
> Walter leaned over, touched Ann's arm gently and whispered, "Pillsbury, all-purpose, isn't it?"
>
> And thus began Walter's life of celibacy.[10]

A man will take your guidance if you use diplomacy and tact. The actual process doesn't matter as long as your needs are being met. If a man needs to believe he is the king of the castle, let him be that king as long as you run the kingdom. Heroes are not born; they are created—and best created by savvy women.

Adoption at the Altar

When they marry, most women adopt a child at the altar, and we have no one to blame but ourselves. Even if not married, women find themselves mothering their partners. This dirty little secret must be exposed so we can make adjustments in our relationships and avoid this outcome. In some cases, we actually create and exacerbate this type of motherly codependence. The process begins when we allow the men in our lives to behave like children, when we care for them without asking them to reciprocate. We enable them to rely on us to do all the tasks they don't want to do or the chores their mothers did for them when they were younger. I have even seen female-male roommates fall into this trap. Do not become a maid or a mother to a grown man!

One of my clients, Ella, shared her frustration about fostering bad habits in her husband early in their marriage and her fear that he had become a lazy monster that could never be rehabilitated. You see, she replaced his mother as far as domestic chores were concerned, and he literally had no household responsibilities. Ella also had a full-time job, so this imbalance in the workload created resentment that showed up by Ella withholding sex as punishment. John was left in a state of confusion because he was behaving as he always had and could not figure out why he was being punished.

I suggested that the solution might be as simple as a conversation that started with the end result in mind. Ella told John that regardless of the past arrangement, she wanted and needed more help at home and she knew two specific things he could do to make a difference. She went on to admit that their sex life had declined because of hidden resentment; she apologized and said that the situation would change that night if he felt comfortable with the new plan. She stressed that this was not an ultimatum but a win-win scenario because she wanted to make love with him and she needed his support to feel passionate. Their relationship could not be better now, and they both feel appreciated.

Often, even the most independent men can't seem to find their own socks at home and will ask us the location of items we haven't even touched. Their needs always seem to be immediate and critical and require them to speak in a louder-than-usual voice with a slightly accusatory tone. Somehow we are responsible for their disorganization. Typically, the last person to move the item was, in fact, the seeker himself.

Interestingly, men seem to function perfectly well during the courting process, yet as soon as they are married to or living with a woman, they regress back to infantlike behavior. If we have a controlling and dominant side, men will quickly relinquish to us all decisions pertaining to selecting restaurants, making personal appointments, dropping off the dry cleaning, and selecting gifts, along with all other miscellaneous tasks they feel women just do better than men. Over time, being in charge at home becomes tiring for women, and we all complain that our husbands don't take romantic initiative. But haven't we created our own problem?

Too often, women become neurotic about minor details such as how the towels are folded and how the dishwasher is loaded. Are we nuts? We can't seriously think that loading the dishwasher requires the special skills of a woman. If men are willing to help, let them. The towels will be folded and the dishes will be cleaned. Focus on something that is actually worth your time instead of being picky about meaningless chores.

I'm sure we've all seen ads that play up the dramatic difference in the way an illness affects a man versus a woman. A case of the flu will incapacitate a virile man, while a woman must go on about her daily duties as if the same flu affects only her pinky finger. This imbalance has been created and allowed by women. We too could just relax on the couch and milk our sickness for everything it's worth. But we don't, and whose fault is that?

A year ago I had surgery that left me bedridden for almost two weeks. My husband said he was more than capable of taking care of me so I would need no additional help. The first day he ordered me a pizza for dinner, put an action movie in the DVD player, and left me while he went surfing for three hours. The second day, he filled a beer cooler with ice cream, soda, and a sandwich—all of which I had no interest in eating—and brought it into the bedroom. He then left for work for several hours. That's when I called my mother to come take care of both me *and* my husband so we could survive those two weeks.

One other way men are like children is that both men and children seem obsessed with the television and can be completely content watching it. The house could be burning down, and most men would watch the television as they run by with the dog and the fire extinguisher in hand. I must admit that I am also fond of the television, but my husband takes his obsession to new levels. We currently have four televisions in our house. We have no patio furniture, the baby's room is not complete, and my husband's office needs a makeover. At dinner last night he had an epiphany and said, "You know what we need? A television in the bathroom. This way I can watch the news in the morning while I'm showering and I'll save time." I looked around the room to see if I was on a hidden-camera show, but unfortunately, that was not the case. I also cannot imagine how my husband extracts pleasure from watching his two favorite shows: *Dirty Jobs* and *Deadliest Catch*. In *Deadliest Catch*, for example, one minute the characters talk intently about the serious dangers that exist in their job and say that a small slip could cause death. The next minute, they are swinging from fish hooks over the side of the boat in freezing water because they are bored. I don't actually watch these shows, but I like them because I have extracted significant sums of money and some grand favors from my husband while he was completely absorbed in them. He just hands me his checkbook to make me go away.

Although it may somehow seem easier to take on a motherly role with your mate, try to use rational judgment about this decision. It is very difficult to teach old dogs new tricks. If you enable your man to be a child, you will eventually grow tired of always being the adult. If you really want to be needed, get yourself a pet.

The F Word

The new F word in the twenty-first century is "feminism," but for now we are focusing on "fidelity." "Thou shalt not covet thy neighbor's wife" seems to be a commandment that can't be followed in our era. What's the solution? Marry a man who loves you just a *little bit* more than you love him. This golden rule of relationships should be provided in a handbook for all females at birth so we would never waste our time trying to change, rehabilitate, and refine rogue men.

I always love receiving confirmation of this rule. In the May 2006 issue of *Real Simple*, Susan Orenstein shared life lessons from women one hundred or more years in age. Mary Cavaliere, a 106-year-old resident of New York, said one of the secrets to her success was to "marry a man who is more in love with you than you are with him." She also declared, "Women are equal to men."[11]

Women will be happiest when paired with men who understand the true definition of "love": understanding, appreciation, and respect. The only good husband is the one who is willing to share the spotlight with you and prefers you to stand in the brightest part of the light. As the Hebrew Talmud states: "Be very careful if you make a woman cry, because God counts her tears. The woman came out of a man's rib. Not from his feet to be walked on. Not from his head to be superior, but from the side to be equal. Under the arm to be protected, and next to the heart to be loved."[12]

Be sure to closely gauge how much more a man loves you because, as you know, respect (one of the qualities of love) is earned. Do not enforce the rule in order to take advantage of a man because he's in love with you—especially if you don't love him. Even so, the rule is the standard that allows you to create lasting happiness. A little more love on a male's part results in fidelity and lasting love.

Interestingly, many men boast of fidelity like it's a badge of honor. They seem to think that they have performed above and beyond society's expectations if they are actually faithful to their wives. Many men tell me that the sacrament of marriage was created when the life expectancy was thirty to fifty years and that humans were never intended to mate for a lifespan of fifty to seventy years.

During the latter part of my pregnancy, my husband came home from a testosterone-filled men's night out at the ballgame. He told me that while he was sitting at the bar next to a friend, the friend quietly inquired, "Are you being faithful to your wife while she's pregnant?" My husband was speechless because he couldn't possibly imagine cheating on his wife—the woman who had ballooned to the size of Shamu the whale all in the name of procreation. When he answered, "Of course I am," his embarrassed friend said, "Oh yeah, so was I."

That same evening, another friend related the escapades that had occurred during a trip he had recently returned from. He proudly declared that although the majority of the men in the group had engaged in secret indiscretions, he was the last good man standing.

Men seem to believe that as long as they acknowledge that "men are pigs," it is okay to behave like pigs. Some of the most intelligent men I know have said that because men and women attach different emotions to sex, it should be acceptable for men to stray. Sex is emotionally meaningless to them, they reason; it is a simple physical need. When I point out their ignorance regarding this issue, they always backtrack, trying to redeem themselves, and say, "I was just kidding." It seems that because I make bold (some might say outlandish) statements about men and women—like "Men are not equipped to make women happy; we need to make ourselves happy"—some men think I might possibly condone infidelity. This conclusion is grossly incorrect.

A woman's intuition should be relied on to detect infidelity in her relationships. If you suspect foul play, you are probably correct. One telltale sign of infidelity is a man questioning your whereabouts and suggesting—seemingly out of the blue—that *you* are being unfaithful. Guilt makes people behave in unusual ways. A cheater who wants his steady relationship to end yet is too cowardly to end it himself, often secretly hopes that his partner is also cheating. That way, the breakup will be mutual and his guilt can be relieved. Usually, his hopes are dashed. I have seen numerous examples of cheaters projecting their bad behavior on the ones who love them most. So, if you are wrongly accused, investigate the accuser.

Remember, where there's smoke there's fire.

I was a very happy person. My wonderful girlfriend and I had been dating for over a year and so we decided to get married. There was only one thing bothering me— it was her beautiful younger sister.

My prospective sister-in-law was twenty-two, wore very tight miniskirts, and generally was braless. She would regularly bend down when she was near me and I always got more than a nice view. It had to be delib-

erate because she never did it when she was near anyone else.

One day her "little" sister called me and asked me to
come over to check the wedding invitations. She was
alone when I arrived, and whispered to me that she had
feelings and desires for me that she couldn't overcome.
She told me that she wanted me just once before I got
married and committed my life to her sister.

Well, I was in total shock and couldn't say a word.
She said, "I'm going upstairs to my bedroom and if you
want one last wild fling, just come and get me."

I was stunned and frozen in shock as I watched her
go up the stairs. I stood there for a moment, then turned
and made a beeline straight to the front door. I opened
the door and headed straight toward my car. Lo and
behold, my entire future family was standing outside all
clapping!

With tears in his eyes, my father-in-law hugged me
and said "We are very happy that you have passed our
little test. We couldn't ask for a better man for our
daughter. Welcome to the family!"

And the moral of this story is: always keep your con-
doms in your car.[13]

I can't tell you how many women have stated, "I knew there
was something going on, but I just didn't want to believe it." If a
man's behavior makes you uncomfortable in any way, it should be
examined and addressed. If a man is overly friendly to your best
friend, your sister, or anyone else close to you, this is a blatant sign
of not only arrogance but disrespect for your feelings. When
women dismiss this type of behavior and pretend that they are

actually pleased that their mate is so fond of their family and friends, they are merely in denial. Following our intuition is an active way to eliminate denial permanently.

Sex: How Much Is Enough?

How much sex is enough sex to keep a man's focus at home? I'm often asked this question by my clients. However, they look at me with disdain upon hearing my answer: "'Nirvana' is three times a week."

Let us refer back to the Law of Three for a moment. According to this law, our thoughts about the kind of relationship we want become our actions. If you want a healthy, balanced relationship, you must be willing to invest in that relationship and take steps toward making it successful. Perhaps you know what steps are necessary—for example, acknowledge your partner more for his household contributions, create a "date night" to show your partner that you appreciate him, or give him more physical contact, including more regular sex. But thinking about and knowing what will make your relationship work is not enough. The Law of Three makes these steps tangible. You first recognize that action is needed, you then decide what specific action will create the best outcome, and you then carry out that action.

A candle loses nothing by lighting another candle.

Erin Majors

Let's face it: in sex, a man's goal is ejaculation, not foreplay. We can usually satisfy this need in a short amount of time. When I remind women of this, they say to me, "Are you suggesting that I have sex even when I don't want to? Doesn't that negate my self-respect?" The answer is no; it is part of nurturing your relationship.

Let me explain. Men have a physical need for sex. Ejaculation "defrags a man's hard drive," so to speak. Think about animals in the wilderness. To them, a sexual release instinctively leads to peak performance. Following sex, they can perform their required duties in the natural world at full capacity. A human man has the same instincts and the same needs, and he operates at his maximum capacity with regular sexual maintenance. Several clients have told me that after months of unsuccessful couple's therapy they started having regular sex with their husbands, and suddenly all their problems were resolved.

Ken Barnes made some interesting observations in his book *Ten Things Women Do to Screw Up a Man's Life*: "In many cases, women think that sex is recreation for a man and refuse to recognize that satisfaction of this urge is a fundamental need. This erroneous belief/conclusion leads women to be comfortable in withholding sex and intimacy when they feel, for whatever reason, their man does not deserve it."[14] He also says, "A man's immediate needs are of no concern to women. Her concern is what is in it for her and the fulfillment of her life-fantasy. His willingness to put a ring on her finger, go to work for 10 hours a day, and put up with a job he dislikes, etc. . . . are all taken for granted."[15]

Strive to have sex an average of twice a week. Once a week is palatable for most men and will certainly put you in the "above normal" category. The majority of women I know personally and professionally have revealed that the norm for them is three times a month. Whether you want to hear this or not, that is just not enough.

Vanessa was appalled when I told the group of women in my seminar that having sex three times a week was optimal for a healthy marriage. She shared that she and her husband had been going to a marriage counselor for six months and this was their third time in therapy in the last five years. I said, "I'm not suggesting that sex is the answer because I obviously don't know your personal and intimate situation, but you've got nothing to lose by trying." The key is to make it natural, not a prescription that you are filling because you were told to. Five weeks later, Vanessa contacted me and said, "It worked. We stopped therapy, and he is now doing what I ask of him without my nagging, and I am even looking forward to sex. Sometimes I even beat your quota and hit four and five times weekly."

Frequent sex is not an exercise in futility but an exercise in relationship maintenance. Let's remember that all partnerships require an investment. You wouldn't expect your friends to understand if you consistently ignored their needs, and you would never dream of ignoring the needs of your children or the people you work with. You know that lasting relationships take work. That same investment and concern must apply to your romantic relationships.

After hearing all of this, women say, "Shouldn't it be easier than this? Shouldn't I *want* to have sex with my husband? I want to maintain my friendships; why can't I feel the same way about sex?" The answer is that we assume that our relationship with our husband won't change, regardless of whether or not we have sex with him. This is a misconception. We need to think about the reason we are nurturing our sexual relationships with our partners: so we can get more of what we want.

We should look on the bright side. We can reserve our positive energy for bonding with other women and focusing on our core values instead of spinning our wheels trying to turn men into our "best girlfriends." Besides, as long as a man is receiving regular sex, he is happy and content. While we attach a lot of emotional substance to our romantic liaisons with our husbands or significant others, we need to know and accept that men feel their relationships are productive when they have an intimate, sexual connection.

The following is a crystallized example of the way men view sex.

Her Diary:
Sunday night I thought he was acting weird. We had made plans to meet at a bar to have a drink. I was shopping with my friends all day long, so I thought he was upset at the fact that I was a bit late, but he made no comment. Conversation wasn't flowing so I suggested that we go somewhere quiet so we could talk. He agreed but he kept quiet and absent. I asked him what was wrong; he said nothing. I asked him if it was my fault that he was upset. He said it had nothing to do with me and not to worry. On the way home I told him that I loved him; he simply smiled and kept driving. I can't explain his behavior; I don't know why he didn't say I love you too. When we got home I felt as if I had lost him, as if he wanted nothing to do with me anymore. He just sat there and watched TV. He seemed distant and absent. Finally, I decided to go to bed. About ten minutes later he came to bed, and to my surprise he responded to my caress and we made love. I still felt that he was distracted and his thoughts were somewhere else. He fell asleep and I cried. I don't know what to do. I'm almost sure that his thoughts are with someone else. My life is a disaster.

His Diary:
Today the Dolphins lost, but at least I got laid.[16]

Creating a hero takes intuition and effort, much like building a masterpiece. It takes a combination of expressing love, leading by example, setting boundaries, and instilling confidence to ensure that your mate is happy and functioning at a high level. Effort does not always equate with success in relationships if your partner is more of a villain than a hero. However, if your mate has potential, it is well worth the investment you put into the relationship.

No Woman Is an Island

EVERY WOMAN MUST CREATE A CAVALRY

The concept of a cavalry has been around for millions of years, yet women seem to prefer to do things the hard way. We willingly embrace the martyr mentality and complain about how much we have to do instead of securing other capable women to help us carry our load.

Every man I have ever talked to about an overload of work and home responsibilities says, "I wish my wife would hire help." They go on to admit, "I can't do the work to her standards, but I'm all for her finding someone who can." So if you can afford it, *hire* a cavalry. If you think you can't afford it, make sure you are properly evaluating that decision. I hired a personal assistant who makes $15 an hour. At first that seemed like a lot to me, but in six hours a week, she accomplishes thirty of my tasks for me so I can spend more time doing things that are aligned with the results I want in my life. I spend $90 a week and feel like I've won the lottery.

If you can't bring yourself to hire a cavalry, at least allow your emotional supporters to step in and help carry some of the weight. These are motivated volunteers who have your best interests at heart and in mind.

You also need to look at life as a game of inches. We need to take one day at a time and enjoy our process instead of being consumed by a to-do list that regenerates itself every day. We do not have to accomplish a week's work in a day, even if we can, and we do not have to get carried away with taking on *all* the responsibility. Allowing our partners and coworkers to contribute less than they should only builds resentment in us. Don't enable people to take advantage of you. Share the work; don't do it all.

> Don't enable people to take advantage of you. Share the work; don't do it all.

Even if we don't do it all, women can have it all. Many of us make the unfortunate assumption that "balance" means a calm, predictable, boring life. However, we will achieve true balance only when we have the confidence to align our inner desires with how we live our lives. The martyr in women tells us that it is irresponsible and unrealistic to even attempt to have it all. This is just a coward's excuse for settling and choosing the life of a flatliner. The truth is that women are better equipped than men to have it all. The difference? Men think they deserve it, and women think they don't.

As part of achieving balance, women need to set expectations and boundaries in any male-female live-in relationship and revisit these at least annually. Women easily fall into domestic roles and take on those responsibilities because we can complete the tasks quicker and more efficiently than men can. However, doing so often creates habits that cannot be broken. One of the hardest things that a woman must do is to have patience and give the man of the house time to complete his chores. The most common and routine excuse we all hear from men is "I was planning to do it, but you were just so impatient you couldn't wait."

I have made healthy compromises with my husband. I have explained to him that although certain chores may seem trivial to him, they are very important to me. For instance, I require the house to be picked up all the time, every day. Friends joke that our home looks like it has constantly been staged for real estate showings. I was raised by an obsessive-compulsive cleaner, so I feel quite balanced in comparison. When we first moved in together, my husband and I struck a deal: he would pick up all his items in all the shared rooms of the house, and in turn, I would do all the laundry. His office and the garage were off limits to my cleanliness. After four months of a smooth transition, he decided to test the boundaries of our deal. When some of his clothes were missing and he had exhausted his search, he finally asked where they might be. I directed him to the trash. He was shocked. I explained that we had made a deal, and I was simply following through on my part of the bargain. Then I asked if he wanted to renegotiate our deal. After a few silent moments and an inquiry into my sanity, he agreed to keep the agreement in place. This "subtle" approach achieved great results.

We Women Need to Stick Together

Women need other women. Unfortunately, we do not always support each other. We need to keep in mind that women do not need to stand trial for every decision they make about motherhood (working versus not working, breast-feeding, discipline, and everything else). In a private setting, almost all women will tell you that the most hurtful criticism comes not from their husbands, boyfriends, and male comrades but from themselves and their peers—other women. If we endorsed each other instead of chastising each other, we would change society's perception of a woman's worth.

Let's stop the insanity. If we could recognize the "real" enemy—the old-school ideas that have defined roles for women—we would see that the best defense is to support and understand each other's choices. If we don't see that, our choice to attack each other instead of fighting for more equality will continue to be a contributing factor in the inequality between men and women. Men don't need to oppress us; we do a very good job on our own.

The reality is that every woman needs her own "wife." This need can be met with a cavalry composed of people filling a wide range of supporting roles, spanning from mothers and best friends to personal assistants and nannies.

> **Working women today are trying to achieve in the work world what men have achieved, but men have always had the help of a woman at home, who took care of all the other details of living! Today, the working woman is also that woman at home.**
>
> *Jeanne Elium*

Putting a cavalry in place will allow us to have it all. Every woman needs to have her own cavalry and be a member of someone else's. The key is to constantly add cavalry members so you always have adequate backup.

Make the decision today to embrace this new way of being. Acknowledge the personal cost of trying to do everything on your own and make an internal commitment to ask for more support. You must be willing to explore collaboration and develop interdependence. Laura Desmond, CEO of Starcom MediaVest Group, the Americas, shares, "One trick you can use to see how far you are in establishing a network outside of your normal comfort zone is to take a look at your BlackBerry. How many names do you have in it today? How many names would you like a couple of years from now? The more you build the database, the more you're getting

comfortable with things outside your territory and therefore leading and having a chance to influence more and more people."[1] You
need support, you deserve it, and it can make your life a lot more
balanced. Besides, your contribution to the world is too valuable to
leave unsupported.

Cavalry Members

A cavalry should include strategic allies, emotional pillars, and
taskmasters, which are described below. Be sure to recruit all three
kinds of members for your cavalry.

Strategic Allies

Strategic allies have the knowledge or skills that can take you to the
next level professionally and personally. They are like-minded
women with whom you can trade support because you complement each other's strengths and weaknesses.

Many of us wrongly assume that when
we request assistance from other women,
they are annoyed because, like us, they are
so busy. Instead, women naturally want to
share their advice because doing so makes
them feel clever, they are proud of having
mastered tricks of the trade, and they love
praise and recognition. Women love to be
complimented for figuring out the best way
to get work done. Acknowledging a woman for her expertise not
only empowers her but puts you in a position to gain abundant
insight.

> **Putting a cavalry in place will allow us to have it all.**

Strategic allies can provide help with household chores, baby-sitting, legal services, travel arrangements, and even attendance at seminars and workshops. Barter is a good way to recruit a strategic ally. I love to trade a seat in one of my seminars for the skills of a strategic ally who will add value to my life. I have received facials, massages, secretarial services, doctor visits, art, and photography. The more creative the trade, the better I like it.

Here are two examples of how the process works. About six months ago, I wanted to increase the exposure my work was getting in my local area of San Diego. I knew that a newspaper editor in town had been meaning to come to one of my seminars but never seemed to find the time for it. I offered her and her assistant admission to one of my seminars free of charge if she would write about it in her paper. The alliance we formed gave both of us something we wanted.

Ronnie works three days a week as a financial planner while her toddler daughter is in a Montessori preschool. While her work is well paid, it is only part-time, and she wanted some help paying the bills. During a conversation with the preschool director, who had a preschooler at home two days during the week, Ronnie proposed a swap: she would provide childcare for the director on the two weekdays that she didn't go to work, and the school would give her a break on tuition fees. The director agreed, and they are both happy with the arrangement.

Emotional Pillars

Emotional pillars are our biggest cheerleaders. They provide a shoulder to cry on and assure us that we are not crazy, just super-human. Emotional pillars offer unconditional love without judgment, any time of the day. The most qualified cavalry member in this regard is, of course, the Bella Momma (your mother). Our mothers know what we feel, think, and desire. They admire us for living better lives than they have chosen. Although they desired a more balanced life, their obstacles were greater, and the light at the end of the tunnel was just a little too dim to see. Our mothers also understand our longing for a moment's peace. These amazing women are just like us with all of our insecurities, guilt, and frustrations about wanting it all and fearing that we may never have it. Never take advantage of your mother, but always take her up on her offers to help.

The mother-daughter relationship is the most complex relationship that exists. Take Melanie, for example. She is a single mother of two teenage girls who works an entry-level job to pay the bills. She wishes she had made different choices when she was younger, so she barks what not to do in her daughters' ears, but when she feels guilty about being too stern, she behaves like the girls' friend as opposed to their mother, which sends mixed messages. Melanie had to learn to refocus her daughters' attention toward what they do want, so their interactions could be based on positive communication versus negative thoughts and words. She now talks about what is possible and how the girls' progress inspires her to do better.

A mother has the almost indescribable responsibility to not only raise her daughter but to lead by example. If she cannot take that lead, then she must find ways to encourage her daughter to do what she could not do. Here's what Ursula M. Burns, president of business group operations at Xerox Corporation, says about her mother: "I actually do believe I came from a background that groomed me to be successful in business. I came from a very poor single-parent household, but from a woman who was extremely confident, very amazing, and had nothing but outstanding expectations of me and my siblings. So while business wasn't the goal, success was the goal. There was no expectation that I would be anything but great at whatever I did. My mother is the person who instilled in me that it is possible and just go after it."[2]

Sometimes when I am standing in front of the mirror, my thoughts wander back to the moments when my mother recited her indefatigable belief in me: "Look how pretty you are. You can even see how smart and confident you are just by looking at you. You will change the world and everyone you meet." I distinctly remember times when I felt very ugly—when I had acne all over my face, was too plump, or sported a mullet hairstyle—and thinking to myself, "My mother seems to be very smart, and she speaks with such conviction. Maybe her words are the reality, and my thoughts are subjective and distorted. I know she's right about most things, so maybe she's right about this." At the time, I didn't appreciate the magnitude of her words, but I am certain that all through life they gave me confidence when I needed it most.

I often wondered if my mother knew how much I adored her. Then something happened that made me think she must know. She was paid the highest compliment by a group of her friends: she was asked to write a book of tips on how to raise a daughter because her female friends wanted their own daughters to feel about them as I obviously did about her.

> **My doctors told me I would never walk again. My
> mother told me I would. I believed my mother.**
>
> *Wilma Rudolph*

Some of us have been burdened with the horrible challenge of not knowing our mother, losing our mother too early, or having a mother who was never taught that blood is thicker than water. Not having this emotional pillar is one of the most heartfelt tragedies that exist for women today. Fortunately, friends also do well in the role of emotional pillars. Sometimes we need another woman to stick up for us in order to recognize our own worth. When women bond, oxytocin is released in their brains.[3] Oxytocin is the same hormone released when we have an orgasm, so calling in the cavalry is like calling in an orgasm. This is why women love and need to network with other women.

Two women spending the day together would never share only a few sentences of conversation. Men, however, would be content to spend the entire day exchanging as few words as possible with each other. Male bonding does not cause them to experience an orgasm.

Note that oxytocin is also released when a woman breast-feeds her baby.[4] She is completely satiated, and all her needs are met; hence the lack of libido and need for connection with her male partner.

Here's a story that illustrates the importance of recruiting emotional pillars for your cavalry. Lynne had been a stay-at-home mom for fifteen years. As her younger child got ready to leave for college, she prepared to reenter the workforce. Her husband was supportive, but as he had never lost momentum in the corporate world, he didn't understand the rocky road Lynne was about to travel. She had extensive interviews and accepted a managerial position at a firm she liked. Before she left the work force, Lynne had been working at the director level, but a managerial position was the best offer she received. She also would be reporting to someone ten years younger than her. She knew she needed some emotional support. That's when Lynne's best friend stepped in and the two began their twice-weekly "interventions." Those discussions and her friend's support helped Lynne stay sane and successfully navigate the twists and turns of her new situation.

The Mother-in-Law. We know that our mothers can be emotional pillars. But do our mothers-in-law fit into our cavalry? That is a good question. Mothers-in-law have been given an incredibly bad reputation, usually based on a mixture of the truth and lots of tall tales spun about evil monsters-in-law whose only goal is torturing their sweet, unsuspecting daughters-in-law. If you have a "monster-in-law," I empathize with you and encourage you to fight the battles you can win.

If you aren't married, I would like to provide some words of wisdom before you encounter the all-encompassing, obsessive adoration that a mother has for her son. First, a critical truth: your husband will play a monumental role in the success or failure of your relationship with your mother-in-law. Women need all the help we can get, so building a relationship with your mother-in-law that adds her to your cavalry is the desired goal. Before you can reach this goal, you and your husband must make one agreement: he must never, in any context, for any reason, share with his mother negative feelings about anything you have said or done. Your mother-in-law will never forget, and she will hold a grudge, which will leave you at a big disadvantage. You must make this agreement with your husband early in your relationship, well before the marriage ceremony, so that this rule will never be broken.

Here are four important mother-in-law tips to consider:

1. Suggest, through positive encouragement, that your husband tell you about any issues that are bothering him before he confides in his mother. If he has personal or professional problems, you need to position yourself as a supportive and nonjudgmental ear he can turn to. This might prevent him from keeping you out of the loop. Simply tell him that you want to build a lasting relationship with your mother-in-law and because all women sometimes overreact to minor circumstances, you would like to help him resolve any issues before his mother gets involved.

2. Never, ever encourage your husband to stop talking to his mother. Doing so is one of the largest marital mistakes you could ever make. Even if he agrees to this initially, he will eventually resent you for lodging a wedge between them.

3. Always acknowledge his mother on her birthday and Mother's Day. Make sure that you subtly show that you participated in the gift process. At the very least, sign the card. You will usually be the one buying the gift or remembering the occasion in the first place.

4. Remember that even though your mother-in-law may like you a lot, she gave birth to your husband. This means that she likes him at least a little bit more than she likes you. A mother always wants to spend some time alone with her child, so do yourself a favor and find a way to make this happen. For example, you might meet your husband and his mother for dinner after they have had cocktails and appetizers together. Stay at work a little late, linger at the grocery store, just find a way to give them a little time alone, even if your husband would rather not have it.

If you follow this advice, chances are that your mother-in-law can be an emotional pillar.

Taskmasters

Taskmasters, in this context, are the cavalry members who help with activities that drain you. For example, hire a nanny, a housekeeper, a personal assistant, or all three.

Many women think they cannot afford taskmasters. Yet in reality, they can't afford not to have them. Alicia, for example, had held managerial positions in the corporate world her whole working life. She was in line to step up to the rank of vice president—one of four candidates for the job and the only woman. She learned through an ally that one potential problem with her being chosen for the position was that she worked flextime hours. Alicia has three children, who need to be fed, driven to and from school, helped with their homework, and taken to various after-school activities. For years she had juggled her children's schedules with her own work schedule because she didn't think she could afford quality childcare. When Alicia made up her mind to actively pursue this lucrative career opportunity, she went to a nanny agency and found a perfect match. She now has a full-time advocate who completes all the tasks that need to be done, which include adoring her children.

A personal assistant can be the star in your universe. The key to having a successful relationship with him or her is to be completely clear about what you want. Tell your assistant, even if you are embarrassed, that you need or want someone to rent out your house, buy your mother's presents, or remember your anniversary. Ask for what you want. Your assistant needs to know exactly what your expectations are so you can get the help you need. Don't tip-toe around your assistant because you don't want to ask too much. That defeats the purpose of having an assistant.

How to Hire Members of Your Cavalry

Be sure to conduct the seven steps of serious due diligence when hiring any member of your cavalry.

1. Check references. A great way to find out a candidate's strengths and weaknesses is by chatting with a reference in a friendly manner; this allows you to get the whole picture.

2. If you're hiring a nanny, meet all the serious candidates twice before you hire anyone. Have at least one trusted friend either recommend or meet them also. This is not required with a housekeeper: one meeting should suffice, but do check references.

3. When it comes to personal assistants, be certain to have lunch or dinner with the candidates. Have cocktails, if appropriate, so you can see them in a social setting. This is required if the assistant will be networking with or for you. Hire on a thirty-day trial basis so you can both see if the relationship is desirable.

4. Personal style is admirable, but your cavalry members' attire should always be in good taste. Your support crew members are a reflection on you. If you are a high-powered business executive and your support team interacts with people whom you must influence, professional attire is mandatory. For a casual environment, relaxed attire should be defined and provocative clothing deemed unacceptable for all environments.

5. Hire people who actually want to do the jobs you need done. An aspiring actress is not a great choice for a housekeeper. Choose someone who wants to be a housekeeper instead.

6. Don't hire the lonely, desperate, or needy; they are too high maintenance and too high risk. Remember: you are hiring someone to support you, not to be another drain on your energy and your time.

7. Finally, and most important, do not hire a woman who is more attractive than you if you are intent on having a serious relationship with a man.

It always amazes me that I must clarify rule number seven. Some of the smartest women have been devastated by ignoring this sage advice. Would you place a hungry lion in a field of gazelle and not expect him to eat? Let me reiterate that the part of the brain that controls instinct is twice as large in men as in women. This is why men desire sex so often. So rule number seven has nothing to do with your self-confidence; it has to do with a man's instinctive sexual drive.

It's not inconceivable that your nanny, your personal assistant, or your housekeeper would like to have your life. She might feel that seducing the man of the house would offer her a ticket to paradise. Don't become your own worst enemy by creating a situation with an unhappy ending. Let me be clear about this: the husband is the person who has everything to risk in this scenario and who would be to blame should he take action on his instinct. However, you would be the one who left out the keys to the candy store.

After you hire your cavalry members, don't think that you're free to do whatever you want and that everything on the home front will be taken care of. Keep in mind that the universe will fill a void. In this life, it is not an eye for an eye; it is an eye for a leg. This means that you have no way of knowing how the consequences of your actions will play out. Gwen has been married for ten years and has a seven-year-old daughter. She loves to go dancing, but her husband prefers to stay at home. Twice a month Gwen and her two girlfriends go out dancing on Saturday night for fun and exercise. Although she wears her wedding ring, she can't help but exchange a few flirtatious glances with men and spend the length of a few songs dancing with them. Her intentions are harmless.

Samuel, Gwen's husband, takes his daughter to a movie twice a month while Gwen is dancing. If asked, Samuel will say that he has no problem with his wife's harmless activity and is just happy that he doesn't have to join her. On one particular Saturday night, he runs into Kara, a mom from his daughter's play group. This single, attractive mother loves the movies and brings her son every

Saturday night. After several coincidental meetings, Samuel and Kara decide to share some ice cream after the movie. This becomes a ritual. The universe is filling a void that has been created with a harmless intention. Samuel's "friendship" escalates to lunch dates, and unintentionally, his fidelity is challenged.

Max often travels on business. He has developed a routine with his wife, Vivian, which involves goodnight phone calls and laughter about the buffoons he works with, his disdain for travel, and how absence makes the heart grow fonder. This is Vivian's favorite part of Max's travel routine. She looks forward to her nightly calls.

One particular evening, Max needed a nightcap after a stressful day. As he was sitting and staring aimlessly at the bar television, an attractive, well-dressed young woman sat next to him. He glanced twice at her because she reminded him of a romantic interest he'd had in college.

She smiled and said, "Do you know me?"

Those were the magic words. Max didn't sleep alone that night, and Vivian didn't receive her phone call. She assumed it must have been a very stressful day.

Concerned but not overly worried, Vivian began the following day with her routine stop at Starbucks. Brian, a man in line behind her, asked if she was driving the white Suburban with the Realtor signs on the side. When she replied yes, they engaged in a robust conversation because he was new in town and was looking for a home immediately. Vivian explained that she and her husband worked together and that she was an apprentice. Her husband was at a convention, she said, but when he returned that evening she would make certain to set up a meeting for the following day.

Max, however, liked having his ego fed with the affections of an attractive stranger, so he decided to stay away one more day. Vivian was understandably disappointed and said she would pick him up at the airport the following morning. That evening, she received a phone call from Brian, who inquired about a meeting and said that his urgency to find a home had escalated. When he found out that Max hadn't returned yet, he asked if Vivian could meet him to simply talk about the area and the best places to start his search. They met for a glass of wine. Vivian loved the attention and couldn't ever remember being so funny. That night she didn't miss the phone call from Max, which he didn't make anyway.

As these stories show, the universe will fill voids. Never hire a support diva as a *replacement* for you. She should always be an adjunct to you and support your efforts to have it all. Leaving your family unattended for long periods of time in the care of another woman is a recipe for disaster. The woman of the house should actually be at the house some of the time. We have no idea in what ways those voids will actually be filled, but we can be certain that they will be filled. If we live every day with the intention to do the very best we can in all of our relationships, including the one with ourselves, the universe will have no void to fill.

A Cavalry Can Keep Us Healthy

What are the health benefits of a cavalry? Assistance with our to-do list minimizes our stress, which can mitigate risk factors that lead to heart disease. Heart disease is the number one killer of women, but it can be controlled through lifestyle changes, including stress reduction.

> It's not our load that breaks us down; it's how we carry it.
>
> Lena Horne

All women need to know that the warning signs of a heart attack include fatigue, shortness of breath, and discomfort in the chest and upper body. One confusing factor is that some of our symptoms, like breaking out in a cold sweat, seem menopausal, so women must take more seriously the responsibility of annual checkups. An annual exam by your ob-gyn is not sufficient to determine heart and other diseases. And the sad fact is, women under fifty are more likely to die of a heart attack than men. The assumed reason is that women don't seek or receive treatment as soon as men.[5]

A cavalry can help us carry our load and reduce the stress in our lives. Why do we need to reduce stress? Sixty-four percent of women who died suddenly of coronary artery disease had no previous symptoms, and 1 in 2.6 U.S. women die of some form of heart disease annually; yet only 9.7 percent of all women think heart disease is the greatest risk to their health.[6]

I spent a significant number of years conducting market research on what women want and what they are concerned about. Heart disease never made the list of concerns.

Menopause

Menopause is a fact of life for all women. Whether you have experienced it yourself; watched your friends, older sisters, mother, or aunts go through "the change"; or enjoyed any of the comedy films centered around the phenomenon of menopause, know that it is inescapable. Knowledge and attitude are critical components when dealing with any transition, and menopause is a transition to be prepared for.

I've seen various versions of the following fictional findings on numerous Web sites and blogs. I'm presenting a distilled version for your enjoyment so we can start this discussion on a light note.

A recent women's health study has revealed that the kind of face and physique a woman finds attractive on a man can differ depending on whether or not she is in menopause. For instance, if she is ovulating, she is attracted to men with rugged and masculine features. However, if she is menopausal, she is more prone to be attracted to a man with scissors lodged in his temple while he is running around on fire. Further studies are expected.

Certain cavalry members best serve us at different times in our lives. Menopause is a time when emotional supporters are critical in maintaining one's sanity.

In my previous career, I focused on women's healthcare and specialized in hormone-related issues. I had the pleasure of working with many women who were in menopause. I have a wide knowledge of both pharmaceuticals and holistic products.

One of the many refreshing truths I discovered is that menopausal women tend to throw subtlety out the window. If you ask them a question, you'll get a direct answer. Based upon my collected data, I have created what I think is a realistic way to be in menopause, which is presented later in this chapter. Some women may think it is arrogant of me to comment about something I have not yet experienced myself. However, I am a woman with a mother in menopause and a fifteen-year background focusing on women's health initiatives.

More than five thousand women in the United States turn fifty every day.[7] Women generally live several years longer than men, so they experience the benefits or detriments of aging longer than men do. Unfortunately, our society has tried to fit square pegs into round holes when it comes to menopause. But one size does not fit all. Our mother's menopause is not our menopause, and categorizing this phase of life with a blanket statement that "this is what most women experience" is not acceptable. Women want and deserve to be treated as individuals. They need to understand the changes in their own lives based on their personal physical and mental conditions.

Like many other women, I think a male physician may not be the best choice for childbirth, menopause, or any other "female-related" issues. This may seem like a bold statement, and I certainly realize that there are some highly qualified male ob-gyns, and I myself have been a patient of some of them. Yet my personal preference is to be advised by someone who actually has walked in my shoes as a woman. I grew up in a very small rural town, so I realize that female doctors may not be available to all women. If that's your situation, at least be certain to find a man in touch with his feminine side. On the other hand, I have met female doctors who are so busy trying to be politically correct in a man's world, they seem to have abandoned their womanhood. They present themselves with a cold, hardened exterior, making their patients feel silly and ridiculous when they inquire about their sincere concerns. Of course, these physicians should be avoided. Never be afraid to switch doctors, and always find a practice that meets your needs. You owe it to yourself and all the people who can't live without you to take your healthcare seriously.

In addition to finding the right doctor, women need to discard the archaic idea that doctors are godlike and start taking charge of their own healthcare choices. Being inquisitive is absolutely mandatory to getting the quality healthcare you require to live a robust life. And Western medicine should not be the only option you consider.

It seems appropriate here to share one of my professional regrets: the failure of an incredible program and educational initiative entitled "Test and Treat." The program was led by two male "female-focused" physicians, Dan Mischell and Leon Speroff. Its focus was to encourage women and the physicians who cared for them to measure estradiol levels when treating menopausal symptoms. Estradiol is the most potent naturally occurring estrogen in a woman's body. The suggested range for estradiol levels was 100–150 picograms per milliliter. A level below 100 did not provide the appropriate bone protection women needed to prevent osteoporosis, and a level above 150 increased the negative side effects of hormone therapy, such as breast tenderness. A simple blood test was required to determine an individual's estradiol level. Medication strength could then be adjusted based upon the results.

This concept allowed women to be treated individually and given the exact dose for their exact needs. It should have changed the way menopause was managed in every female patient; however, the process was time-consuming and a little costly, and oftentimes both doctors and women didn't want to make the effort to have this optional test administered. Request this test from your own doctor, or encourage someone you care about to have her estradiol levels checked.

Shall We Dance?

My theory on menopause is that women fall into one of two categories: they dance a fiery tango or an enchanting waltz.

The Fiery Tango. In a fiery tango, women examine their lives and although they know quite a lot, they realize they still have much to learn. They begin to recognize how much they have sacrificed. Even if they would make the same choices again, they long for missed opportunities and lost time. Some decide that they have been treading water for twenty years, juggling ten balls at once in

the pursuit of everyone else's happiness. Their decision to stop juggling may come as quite a shock to the other people in their lives,
who, after twenty years, probably expected the well of giving to
never dry up. Fiery tango women want to discuss their menopause
as a way of dealing with their physical, emotional, and mental
changes. They might tell a male clerk in the grocery store that even
though he is very handsome, their sweating and flushed face is a
result of a hot flash, not his hot body. They are willing to try various techniques and remedies—both traditional and holistic—to
seek relief from their physical symptoms.

Some women, more than you'd think, decide to leave their
husbands after twenty-five or more years of marriage and just be
on their own. For example, when Erin hit the magical age of forty-
five, she was experiencing perimenopause, and the one thing she
craved was the single life. This most often occurs because women
feel that they have completed their responsibilities. Their children
are grown, living successful, fulfilled lives, with children of their
own. They are tired of being *needed* rather than *wanted*, and if their
male partner has not appreciated their contributions, they fear-
lessly move on to a BBD (bigger, better deal). Make no mistake: a
BBD is not another man. It is the freedom to look after only yourself, of never again having to hear "Honey, what's for dinner?"
"Where are my socks?" "What are we doing this weekend?"

All three cavalry categories can be critical to us now. We need
nonjudgmental support from emotional pillars; we want people to
do things for us for a change, so taskmasters are invaluable; and
partnerships with strategic allies can allow us to explore talents
that we may have tabled for years.

I met a fabulous woman while I was writing this book. In her
youth she was a personal assistant and a statuesque beauty who had
an exciting life dating many celebrities, including Joe DiMaggio
(before Marilyn). In menopause she decided to be "man-free" and

self-sufficient, but she also needed a project to be excited about. She answered my ad for a stenographer and became completely engaged in this book. She attended my seminars, and we traded for typing services. She also committed to becoming and staying a deliberate creator. It is never too late to start focusing your life.

As the following example clearly shows, a fiery tango equates to liberation of women from the judgment and constraints that others try to impose on them.

> A woman in her mid-sixties was at home, happily jumping on her bed and squealing with delight.
>
> Her husband watched her for a while and asked, "Do you know how ridiculous you look? What's the matter with you?"
>
> The woman continued to bounce on the bed and said, "I don't care. I just came from my mammogram, and the doctor says I have the breasts of an 18-year old!"
>
> The husband asked, "What did he think about your 68-year-old ass?"
>
> "Your name never came up," she replied.[8]

Enchanting Waltz. The enchanting waltz is an extremely different transition than a fiery tango. These women acknowledge that one phase of their life has been successfully completed and a new phase has started. They embrace change as a welcome chapter in their cycle of life. Even though they may be frustrated by uncertainty about what lies ahead, they have relieved themselves of much female insecurity on their journey to menopause.

Columnist Frank Kaiser once eloquently praised this kind of woman. He described how he admired their self-assurance and their forthright honesty about where you stand with them. He also praised their psychic abilities: "You never have to confess your sins to an older woman . . . they always know." Then he contrasted these wonderful older women with their male counterparts: "For every stunning, smart, well-coiffed babe of 75 there's a bald, paunchy relic in yellow pants . . . making a fool of himself with some 22-year-old waitress."[9]

Women who fall into the enchanting waltz category focus on "paying it forward." They let go of female competitiveness and can be generous cavalry members. They admire and love everything that is unique and different. They feel a sense of liberation as they drink two mimosas for breakfast, linger with a glass of wine over lunch, and eat chocolate cake for dinner. Although they may feel some regrets, women in this peaceful transition gracefully try to touch as many lives as possible. They have no desire for dramatic events or ego gratification, just a peaceful optimism. They are comfortable in their own skin. This feeling is a distinct characteristic of women who dance the enchanting waltz and a sign that their longing for self-definition is complete.

> **You don't get to choose how you're going to die or when; you can only decide how you're going to live now.**
>
> *Joan Baez*

Whatever stage of life you're in, the most significant benefit of having a cavalry is being able to cover all your bases so you can put yourself first. I can't reiterate often enough that putting yourself first is the least selfish thing you can do for others. A cavalry will release your guilt and allow you to invest in yourself. We often treat our pets better than we treat ourselves—with regular trips to the groomer and vet and lavish attention every day. We feel selfish when we want to spend money on an empowerment seminar or a girls' day out or a little pampering. Men don't think twice about joining a fishing trip or a golf game because they actually know how to put themselves first—sometimes too often.

Everyone needs a support crew. Having one is the best way you can do it all. Women who operate on the basis of "My mother did it all without help, so why shouldn't I?" are just plain crazy.

Women Must Master the Three Cs

CONFIDENCE, CREDIT, AND COMFORT WITH SUCCESS

In order to master the three Cs of confidence, credit, and comfort, every woman needs to understand the obstacles and enemies that exist regarding success.

Competitive Feminism

Competitive feminism is the most destructive culprit in women's attempts to reach the top of the corporate ladder and achieve the best results in life. It is the proverbial wolf in sheep's clothing because if someone looks like a woman, shouldn't she behave like a woman? It is the tragedy of female-female relationships.

The following example shows one woman's experience dealing with competitive feminism. Cora was an efficient office manager who had "ruled the roost" for a long time. Her skills were well-honed, and she was definitely the woman in charge of the office. Her supervisor hired Rita as a manager in the grocery department. Rita was eager to please. She was smart and friendly and an efficient multi-tasker. Her goal was to add as much value as possible and simply get along with the rest of the staff. Her looks become her detriment. Cora ignored Rita's ability and decided that she had been hired and would eventually be promoted based on her looks alone. This ignited competitive feminism, and unconsciously Cora began sabotaging Rita's efforts. Rita had experienced this situation before, however, and was prepared with a strategic plan to keep her enemies close. Instead of antagonizing Cora or complaining about her, Rita went out of her way to be cordial and helpful to Cora. Additionally, Rita befriended Cora's subordinates so she could learn the tactics that were being developed behind her back.

At Rita's six-month review she displayed confidence by diplomatically addressing the obvious tension that existed between the two women. She used her emotional intelligence to make a simple statement: "If I have done anything to offend you in any way, I would like to apologize and resolve the matter so we can work together more efficiently in the future." Rita's efforts paved the way for an open dialogue and positive working relationship between the two women.

Mommy Wars

The "Mommy Wars" is the most pronounced example of competitive feminism and should fall into the category of best jokes that women play on each other. Many mothers are giving motherhood a bad name with their frequent judgmental opinions and petty need to compete with other women. Why? Didn't our mothers teach us that those who live in glass houses shouldn't throw stones? Do we really believe that our own lives are so perfect that we can judge the choices of another woman? We are the only beings who understand what it is like to be the "glue" that keeps a family together, yet we smear dirt on the choices of our sisters.

Yolanda was an opinionated "know-it-all" who had been raised by a stay-at-home mom. She staunchly believed that following in her mother's footsteps was the best course of action for her and her own children. She was also a self-proclaimed expert on everything relating to caregiving and would often judge and admonish anyone who deviated from her own parenting style.

Janice, on the other hand, was a working mother who also had been raised by a stay-at-home mom. However, she felt that a job outside the home would provide her children a balanced upbringing and the finances to provide the extras to make their lives better, although she was secretly insecure regarding her choice because she felt guilty about leaving her children with a babysitter.

Yolanda and Janice met at their husbands' office Christmas party. As the conversation between the two of them progressed, Yolanda fell into her role as judge, jury, and preacher. Instead of retreating into polite social agreement, Janice became fully engaged in emotionally charged banter. The conversation led to which children would turn out better as they reached adulthood. Yolanda was startled to realize that she had become so caught up in daily tasks that she didn't give her children any more quality time than Janice gave her children. Choice is one of the most critical parts of motherhood. All of us need to decide the best course of action for our own family based on our particular situation, resources, and beliefs. No matter how committed a man says he is to being a parent, the majority of responsibility will always lie on the shoulders of the mother. We must support each other in order to escalate the value of motherhood to the highest level.

There is a special place in hell for women who don't help other women.

Madeleine Albright

Thousands of books have been written about pregnancy and motherhood, but I have discovered a dirty truth that none of them mention. Misery wants company in motherhood. Everyone warned me to ignore the horror stories of violent morning sickness, torturous labor, and tyrannical toddlers. Yet no one informed me of the cunning ways that we clever women torment unsuspecting first-time mothers.

As I write this book, I am eight months pregnant. Fortunately, I have been blessed with an amazing pregnancy—no morning sickness, no nausea, and a high energy level. However, I never discuss that in mixed company. Even women who claim to be my friends find it impossible to let me wander in joyful denial through my pregnancy. According to them, a typical pregnancy results in breast-feeding exhaustion, postpartum depression, or a colicky baby. But they can't break my spirit. My revenge is to remain naively optimistic, which torments these women.

The fundamental difference between me and them is that I have already learned to create a cavalry so I don't have to "do it all." I have hired a housekeeper and a part-time nanny, and I've persuaded my mother to stay for three months after the baby is born. I'm sure my transition into motherhood will be blissful chaos.

One reason that motherhood is a tough job is because women are automatically *expected* to be good mothers. It is supposed to just come naturally. Evidently, having breasts and a vagina means you have all the knowledge required for being a good parent. I find it humorous when a man is complimented on being a great father. If you ask why the praise was given, the answer is always "He spends time with his kids." Can you imagine calling a woman a "great mother" just because she spends time with her kids? So why wouldn't women stick together in the face of all the absurd inequities that exist?

One of my male clients shared an interesting opinion with me. He happens to be a psychologist, and he told me that he had a simple way to describe the difference between a mother and a father. He said that in a life-or-death situation where a choice had to be made, almost all women would choose their children over their husbands and almost all men would choose their wives.

One of the real advantages that men have over women is that they are born with a fierce loyalty to each other. Men will never throw each other under the bus, but women will run you over, baby in hand, and keep on going. Here's an all-too-true illustration of this difference:

Friendship between Women:
A woman doesn't come home one night. The next day she tells her husband that she had slept over at a girlfriend's house. The husband calls his wife's 10 best friends. None of them know anything about it.

Friendship between Men:
A man doesn't come home one night. The next day he tells his wife that he had slept over at a friend's house. The woman calls her husband's 10 best men friends. Eight of them confirm that he had slept over, and two claim that he's still there.[1]

A talented young man once worked for me as a department director. He had an opening in his department, and many qualified candidates applied. However, he said he personally knew the individual who was the perfect fit for the job. He handed me the man's resume, which supplied no information that qualified him for the position. In fact, he appeared to be very much underqualified for the job. Puzzled, I inquired about the director's rationale for his recommendation. The director pontificated on and on about what a great person his friend was and, more importantly, what a talented coach he was for the local softball team. He also added that his friend was the best surfer in their Saturday morning surf club. As I silently stared at him across my desk, I smiled at his arrogance. I wondered if a woman would be so audacious as to endorse a friend as a qualified candidate on the basis of friendship alone.

When the director's friend was not hired, my employee held a childlike grudge for six months, critiquing every move the new hire made. What astonished me most was that my employee had no regard for how his decision might have hurt his own reputation. This example of professional suicide demonstrates the lengths that men are willing to go in the spirit of peer endorsements.

I admire the bold steps that men will take in defending each other. Women, on the other hand, would hardly ruffle their petticoats to support another woman's endeavor unless she had all the necessary qualifications.

How can we earn the respect and support of men in our struggle for equality when we can't even support each other? I have all I can do to make the right choices for my own family, let alone impose my choices upon another woman. The most important responsibility for any of us as mothers is to be happy with our choices so that we exude confidence in all we do—whether this means working in an office or staying at home. If we keep our sanity and self-worth, won't we be better parents?

Today's women have become so stressed about making the right choices regarding motherhood that we try to create a fixed schedule for childbirth. Unfortunately, life doesn't happen on a fixed schedule, and there is no best time to procreate. The longer we work before childbirth, the more likely our careers will advance and the less perceived time we will have for motherhood. On the contrary, we could argue that having babies early in our careers and temporarily leaving the work force is the best decision, yet when we reenter, we must compete with technologically advanced youth who make us feel outdated.

Should I suggest that moms who stay at home all day become so tired of the *Groundhog Day* routine that they resort to using television as a babysitter, scheduling constant play dates for their children's entertainment, and sneaking drinks of wine from sippy cups so they can get intoxicated in order to tolerate the boredom of mundane conversations? Should I say that working mothers fool themselves when they claim that childcare makes their children more adaptable in society? Or should I simply shut up and mind my own business until I'm named "Mother of the Decade"?

An empowered woman chooses if and when she wants to have kids based on her individual situation and resources. Regardless of how attentive the man is in her life or his verbal commitment to participate in child rearing, the majority of the parenting responsibility falls upon the mother. So a woman needs to determine if her heart and soul are ready by evaluating her particular circumstances. If the answer is yes, nothing else matters. A woman committed to a child will make all the difference in that child's life, and she will move mountains to ensure a wonderful life. That life may include day care, nannies, or Mom's full attention at home, but decisions need to be made based on the best outcome for that family, regardless of others' opinions.

POSITION: Mother, Mom, Mommy, Mama, Ma
JOB DESCRIPTION: Long term, team players needed, for challenging, permanent work in an often chaotic environment. Candidates must possess excellent communication and organizational skills and be willing to work variable hours, which will include evenings and weekends and frequent 24 hour

shifts on call. Some overnight travel required, including trips to primitive camping sites on rainy weekends and endless sports tournaments in faraway cities. Travel expenses not reimbursed. Extensive courier duties also required.

RESPONSIBILITIES: The rest of your life. Must be willing to be hated, at least temporarily, until someone needs $5. Must be willing to bite tongue repeatedly. Also, must possess the physical stamina of a pack mule and be able to go from zero to 60 mph in three seconds flat in case, this time, the screams from the backyard are not someone just crying wolf. Must screen phone calls, maintain calendars and coordinate production of multiple homework projects. Must have ability to plan and organize social gatherings for clients of all ages and mental outlooks. Must be willing to be indispensable one minute, an embarrassment the next. Must handle assembly and product safety testing of a half million cheap, plastic toys and battery operated devices. Must always hope for the best but be prepared for the worst. Must assume final, complete accountability for the quality of the end product. Responsibilities also include floor maintenance and janitorial work throughout the facility.

POSSIBILITY FOR ADVANCEMENT & PROMOTION: Virtually none. Your job is to remain in the same position for years, without complaining, constantly retraining and updating your skills, so that those in your charge can ultimately surpass you.

PREVIOUS EXPERIENCE: None required unfortunately. On-the-job training offered on a continually exhausting basis.

WAGES & COMPENSATION: You pay them! Offering frequent raises and bonuses. A balloon payment is due when they turn 18 because of the assumption that college will help them become financially independent. When you die, you give them whatever

is left. The oddest thing about this reverse-salary scheme is that
you actually enjoy it and wish you could only do more.
BENEFITS: While no health or dental insurance, no pension, no
tuition reimbursement, no paid holidays and no stock options
are offered, this job supplies limitless opportunities for personal growth and free hugs for life if you play your cards right.[2]

And do I dare mention the unspoken pressure to give birth to
a male heir? Before my amniocentesis, which determines a baby's
sex with 100 percent accuracy, everyone assumed I was having a
girl. (I, too, had decided that a female likeness would be my next
creation.) This assumption was based on the scuttlebutt, spoken
behind my back, that I am a feminist.

When the news that I was carrying a boy was announced, both
my husband and I were in complete shock. Then I began to receive
the oddest comments. "Your husband must be so happy." "Lucky
you, you're getting the boy out of the way first." "Well, the pressure's off, so you can relax." I was unprepared for all of these comments and, quite frankly, offended. I wondered if my mother felt
inadequate because she had a baby girl first. Did she feel the
intense pressure to have a boy on her second time around? Are we
all lying when we say, "We just want a healthy baby; that's all that
matters."

Japan's Princess Masako certainly understands this pressure.
An entire article in *People* magazine focused on her distress about
a dynasty on the brink of extinction. She and her husband, the
crown prince, had a daughter in 2001 but have no male heir. The
Japanese imperial family was in a quandary about whether or not
to allow a female to ascend the thrown. Princess Masako was so
stressed that she chose to withdraw from public life. Rumors
reported a nervous breakdown.[3] It is unimaginable to me that a

female would not be embraced as an ascendant to the throne, but I must also remember that I live in a country that has not yet been ready for a female president.

Queen Bee Syndrome

Another obstacle to success and another form of competitive feminism is the "Queen Bee Syndrome." This syndrome allows only the queen herself to be successful; in fact, she actually prevents any female worker bees from potentially assuming her role, sometimes resorting to sabotage. It takes hold of a woman when she has clawed and scratched her way to the top of the corporate ladder. She has so many dings in her armor by then and has licked so many deep wounds that she wants to sit on her throne alone. We find it hard to blame a queen bee for her attitude because we know her journey to the throne has been arduous. In fact, queen bees are just trying to protect their territory.

If we were to follow our "natural behavior," we would identify with other women and not compare ourselves to others as men do. A man would never take advice from someone in a "lower" position than himself. He automatically assumes that if the person *knew* more, he or she would *have* more and be in a higher position of authority. Most men also equate financial success with intelligence. They assume that wealthy people must be pretty smart to have all that money and if they appear to be dumb or just not the sharpest pencil in the drawer, they are actually stealthy and cunning; their lack of intelligence is an act to gain a competitive edge.

Women naturally can identify with others, regardless of their status. We have the intuition to know who is genuine and who has helpful guidance to make our lives easier. If we choose to identify with each other more often, we will have more women supporting us, watching our backs, and holding the ladder so we never fall.

Some of us have great runways already built for us. If you have one, take off! But if you don't have one, realize it is your responsibility to grab a shovel and build one for yourself and for those who will follow after you.

Amelia Earhart

How can women start identifying with each other and get ahead? The best way for women to take their rightful place at the top of corporations is through the staunch endorsement and support of those of us who have played the corporate game and won. We must have mercy on the souls of those who will follow behind us and stop the hazing mentality. More women need to support other women.

What Must Women Learn to Achieve Success?

If you're reading this book from beginning to end, you've already learned many of the lessons you need to succeed:

- Why the only ceiling that exists is the one we build
- How to tie multitasking to our core values
- The strength of our emotional quotient
- How to take the lead in our relationships with men
- How to create a cavalry

If you jumped right in to principle 5 first, be sure to read the other chapters as well. The lessons that we still need to learn are as follows:

- ❑ How to set and achieve SMART goals
- ❑ How to confront issues, not people—the fine art of negotiation
- ❑ How to build and show confidence
- ❑ Why we need to take credit for our achievements
- ❑ How to laugh at ourselves and get comfortable with success

Setting SMART Goals

SMART goals have been in existence as long as the laws of nature, yet oftentimes we want to recreate the wheel and ignore standards that have guaranteed success. All goals have to meet the SMART criteria or they should not be set at all. Each of our goals has to be *specific, measurable, attainable, realistic,* and *time sensitive.*

A well-thought-out SMART goal might be "I want seven new quality clients within the next ninety days." This goal meets each criterion that is required to achieve results. It would be ineffective to simply say, "I want to attract new clients." Another common un-achievable goal is "I want to lose weight." A SMART version of that goal might be "I will lose ten pounds in ninety days by exercising four times a week and reducing my intake by three hundred calories a day." The more detailed you can be about what you want and what you are willing to sacrifice to get it, the more attainable your goal will become.

SMART guidelines can also be incorporated in building personal and professional relationships. Your goal might be "I will improve my communication with my children by spending one hour per day discussing their thoughts and feelings and inquiring about ways I can help them achieve their goals." A professional goal might be "I will have one networking lunch per week with a subordinate, peer, or superior to build my collection of contacts for future needs."

Negotiation

The only time you need to think like a man is when it comes to negotiation. Confront issues, not people. Women tend to wear their hearts on their sleeves, and not only does this trait not serve them in the negotiating arena, but it wastes time and energy. Facts are facts and should be treated that way. A negotiation that involves emotion rarely reaches an equitable settlement; oftentimes, one party feels misrepresented.

The majority of men can deal with the issues at hand without emotional attachment. They can leave a negotiation and still meet each other later for a beer. Women may leave feeling downtrodden and emotionally scarred. The most successful women understand that at work—and even in negotiations at home and elsewhere—a steely approach represents their own best interests. Remember that the fool speaks first. Too often, women steer a conversation or a negotiation in the wrong direction by saying too much. Always give your counterpart the opportunity to speak first so you can gather your thoughts and determine your next move.

There is one exception to this approach. During negotiation, we need to call upon our emotional quotient and intuition to decipher the unspoken signs. A woman needs to use *emotional vocabulary* to communicate her point. Let me explain. If you are losing a verbal battle, seek the truth and agree with it. For example, when frustrations heighten, mention that fact to bring the tone of the conversation to a calmer balance. "I can see you're frustrated, and that was not my intention. I simply wanted to make my point. Let me try to explain it in a different way."

If you are negotiating with another woman, disarm rampant emotions very quickly. Redirect the conversation back to the facts with a straightforward approach. Simply state, "This is not about you personally and has nothing to do with how I think or feel about you. These are simply the facts of the situation that we must resolve together."

The ability to resolve conflicts is a strength all women can easily master. Practicing gentle, disarming confrontation will hone our skills and allow us to naturally detach from emotional responses. We need to exchange viewpoints and always use analogies when we are trying to relate with another woman. This will allow her to identify with us and understand our point of view. Women need to realize the positive sides of conflict. Conflict is the route of change and allows personal growth. It directly addresses the issue at hand. Following conflict resolution, unity can be reestablished as illustrated in the following example.

Carol had been promoted to a director-level position, which represented a big jump in responsibility. Her first task was to hire her own replacement. She made an emotional choice based on whom she liked rather than who would best do the job. Within two months, her bad hiring decision had impacted many parts of the company. When Carol's direct supervisor addressed this problem with her, she became very defensive. She immediately called a meeting with the new hire and blamed the woman for making Carol look bad.

Afterward, she realized that she had handled both interactions poorly. She regrouped and asked for a meeting with her boss. This time she showed some professional vulnerability, admitting that she wanted to do everything right and that she was disappointed in herself. She asked for guidance on how to best handle the situation. Her boss helped her establish a plan of action, and the new hire was assessed for her skills and moved to another department where she added value. Carol learned lessons on hiring the right person for the role, she regained her boss's respect, and they worked together from then on.

The Three Cs

The secrets to success can be whittled down to three simple yet complex *C* words: confidence, credit, and comfort. Each can be instilled or learned, but it is the combination of all three that makes good women great.

The importance of self-exploration needs to be addressed before the three Cs can have maximum impact. For example, when selecting a college, living location, or job, you need to please yourself first rather than consider everyone else's agendas. To truly follow your intuition, you need to engage in self-exploration. What are you naturally good at? What comes easily to you? When do you really feel like you're adding value to a discussion or a cause? Regarding self-exploration, Nancy Peretsman, managing director and executive vice president of Allen & Co., shares, "The early years of work are often about going through the journey of figuring out what it is you are most comfortable with. What are your own comparable advantages or distinguishing characteristics? What kind of environments do you like? Where do you work best, and where are you going to thrive?"[4]

Be proud and unwavering about your values and standards. When you develop a set of standards that represent your self-integrity, you need not compromise or feel defensive when you are challenged: you know these standards support your own and others' best interests. When you know who you are, you will attract like-minded people who will respect and appreciate your self-confidence and individuality.

Those like-minded people include men. Picking a mate is so much easier and clearer once a woman chooses to champion herself. Only when she has mastered self-respect should she choose a mate for life. When we need to make decisions, the pleaser in us automatically tells us what will make everyone else happy. We often give our boyfriends' or husbands' opinions equal validity with our own desires, but this is a mistake. Accept guidance from others only when it makes sense to you. This path to making courageous decisions will serve you well.

Remember that nothing has meaning until you give it meaning. Filter out the naysayers' opinions. Misery loves company, and such opinions probably come from those who never had the courage or confidence to pursue their own dreams.

Yes, everyone who ventures into the unknown is scared, but if the path is leading you toward growth, the journey will build character. Women need to have a "whatever it takes" attitude to make their dreams come true, and only with that attitude will they develop the strong self-integrity to defend their choices with no regrets. Staying close to home or following your man are fine decisions if you make them deliberately. Otherwise, they are cowardly choices. Someone will be the first female president of the United States. Why can't it be you? (Unless Hillary beats you to it.)

> **I think the reward for conformity is that everyone likes you except yourself.**
>
> *Rita Mae Brown*

Search inside yourself and decide what level of risk you are comfortable taking. In addition, network with women who have walked the walk in environments that interest you. They can provide invaluable insights. Meeting them could mean volunteering, taking an interesting woman to lunch, joining a nonprofit, taking a class, or joining a women's group. Identify a company that specializes in your area of interest. Within that company, research successful women who have excelled in the particular field that intrigues you. Interview them and inquire about the pros and cons of their position, as well as their road to success.

In your self-exploration, read biographies about women who have changed the way we think about a woman's contributions, and learn whatever you can from the accounts of their lives.

Look at your life as though every opportunity is open to you, as it is to men. Try to examine every aspect of yourself that you possibly can. Try on all this world has to offer, and when you find something you love, acknowledge yourself for discovering it. You can love something else down the road. There is always more, much more, waiting for you.

> Look at your life as though every opportunity is open to you, as it is to men.

So what is success to the modern woman? Millions of studies, articles, books, and summations on this topic all lead to these simple points:

- ☐ Understanding, appreciation, and respect
- ☐ Peace of mind: living one's definition of balance
- ☐ Financial independence
- ☐ A position of responsibility with continuing growth
- ☐ Physical and mental fitness
- ☐ Equality between men and women

Just for comparison, I wanted to share the following excerpt from a list of guidelines written for male supervisors of women in the workforce during World War II. Although we have not achieved our goal of equality, we have made progress.

Tips on Getting More Efficiency out of Women Employees

- Pick young married women. They usually have more of a sense of responsibility than their unmarried sisters, they are less likely to be flirtatious . . .
- When you have to use older women, try to get ones who have worked outside the home at some time in their lives. Older women who have never contacted the public have a hard time adapting themselves and are inclined to be cantankerous and fussy . . .
- General experience indicates that "husky girls"— those who are just a little on the heavy side—are more even tempered and efficient than their underweight sisters . . .
- Give every girl an adequate number of rest periods during the day. You may have to make some allowances for feminine psychology. A girl has more confidence and is more efficient if she can keep her hair tidied, apply fresh lipstick and wash her hands several times a day . . .
- Be reasonably considerate about using strong language around women. Even though a girl's husband or father may swear vociferously, she'll grow to dislike a place of business where she hears too much of this.
- Get enough size variety in operator's uniforms so each girl can have a proper fit. This point can not be stressed too much in keeping women happy.[5]

What are the obstacles to a woman's success?

☐ Martyr mentality: preconceived idea of a woman's role
☐ Work environment biased toward men
☐ Lack of support from family or significant other

As I've said before, not only is putting ourselves first the least selfish thing we can do for others, but it gives women so much more to give back. If you have a lack of support from your family or your significant other, let that be the fuel that feeds your desire to succeed. Don't allow their fear to paralyze you and keep you from your dreams. Remember that sometimes people don't want you to achieve your goals because it would be a constant reminder to them that they didn't take initiative in their own lives. They may also have the selfish concern that your road to success will leave them behind.

Confidence

When a woman who lacks confidence achieves a position of power, she believes she's a fraud and that if anyone found out she wasn't actually qualified for her position, she would be exposed and let go. This is ridiculous. Most of the time, women are over-qualified for their jobs, and the only people who don't believe it are those women themselves. The only ceiling that exists is the one we set for ourselves. Every smart man knows that a smart woman can do his job better, and that's why he has a female advocate at home or at work with his best interests in mind. Remember that you will always be paid according to the job you do, how well you do it, and the difficulty of replacing you.

Even men have this problem concerning confidence. I bought a congratulatory lunch for a very good male friend when he was promoted to vice president. I joked that I had called the restaurant in advance to check the door measurements to make sure his inflated ego could fit in the room. He leaned in close and in a low voice said, "I'm just one day away from delivering furniture." As I laughed, I noticed that he was serious. And he went on to say, "Every day as I exit the elevator, I walk to my office feeling completely naked because I have no idea what the hell I'm doing. I'm just banking on being able to fool the powers that be long enough to figure it out."

Women possess the most valued leadership qualities that confidence encompasses:

- ☐ Sincerity: concern for the betterment of the whole
- ☐ Competence: the ability to get things done
- ☐ Integrity: honesty with oneself and others
- ☐ Intelligence: the ability to organize, plan, and execute while solving problems
- ☐ Courage: determination and guts

All of us, male or female, tend to wonder if we are really qualified when amazing opportunities present themselves. Self-doubt is human, and women must realize that this feeling is not exclusive to them. The key is to keep this insecurity to oneself and not broadcast it to the masses.

> **Courage is very important. Like a muscle, it is strengthened with use.**
>
> *Ruth Gordon*

Women need to at least "fake it until we make it." If we don't, we will never achieve the goals that are naturally ours for the taking. By "faking" it, I mean using bravado as a tool until you develop more confidence. The younger you are, the more bravado you will need, but once you master the corporate ropes, using the tips outlined below, your innate leadership abilities will kick in. It's in our blood.

Although I refer to corporations, I realize that not every woman wants to be a CEO. The following advice applies to your dream, whatever that might be: to become an entrepreneur, an actress, a politician, or mother of the year.

Always Be Overprepared. Never walk into a situation cold when you have time to prepare because that would demonstrate laziness and arrogance. You are your brand, a walking billboard for you. Take this responsibility seriously. It takes only a minute to make a first impression—good or bad. When you see smooth, poised presenters who seem to have a knack for public speaking, that is practice made perfect. Never underestimate the confidence that preparation can provide.

Here are ten presentation tips that demonstrate preparation:

1. Start by thanking your host for the opportunity to speak to the group.
2. Dress for your audience; this will make them more comfortable and more receptive to what you have to say.
3. Outline the presentation so the audience knows what to expect: "Today we have three objectives" or "Today we will discuss five areas of interest."
4. Rehearse your presentation a minimum of three times, even if you are talking for one minute.
5. Rehearse out loud using a hand-held recorder so you can confirm that your points have clarity.
6. If you are a physical talker (you move your hands, use facial expressions, or pace), always practice in front of a mirror to be certain your body language aligns with your message.
7. In any presentation over ten minutes long, use props, visual aids, and a story about yourself that connects you with the topic or the audience.
8. Ask questions or pose situations that the members of the audience can relate to—for example, "Do you ever wish you had an owner's manual to make life simpler?"

9. For presentations longer than thirty minutes, raffle off an item that relates to your topic and makes you memorable—for example, a book, a journal with an applicable quote on the cover, or a service you provide.

10. Always tell the audience how to get more information, thank them for their attention, and end with a memorable quote.

Be Your Own Devil's Advocate. Ask yourself every hard question that could be raised and find answers if you don't already have them. Don't live in a vacuum. Ask someone you respect to troubleshoot with you and see what questions he or she comes up with.

A surefire way to show confidence is to raise the tough questions yourself before others have a chance. This demonstrates that you are thorough and have the foresight to plan for the unknown. Say something like, "As I prepared my presentation, I played devil's advocate, so I want to share obstacles as well as opportunities. You will see that the benefits far outweigh the risks, but it is important for us to consider all angles." Or simply say, "Some of you may be asking yourself about the competition, which is not only prudent but critical, so let me walk you through my analysis." It is so much easier to operate from the offense versus the defense, so answer the hard questions before they are asked.

You can build confidence by simply putting yourself in the naysayers' shoes. Remember that many people wake up every day with the glass half empty. Don't let their negativity ruin your positive momentum.

Admit What You Don't Know. Nothing looks worse than you fumbling for an answer that you obviously don't have. This can ruin all the progress you might have made up until that point. I could not be more serious about this. You could give a solid one-hour presentation and negate the entire effort with unprepared answers. If you know part of an answer, say that and share what you know; otherwise, say, "I don't have the complete answer at this time, so let me get back to you." Then get back to the person as soon as possible. Also invite your teammates to share different information they may have. For example, if someone asks a question and you don't know the answer, show confidence by asking your coworkers, "Do any of you want to jump in and provide your insight?" This way you are not putting any one particular person on the spot.

Get Organized. A critical step to success is figuring out what works for you regarding organization. A cluttered office reflects a cluttered mind. It is critical that your files, your office, your work, and your life have a semblance of order. If you think you are comfortable with chaos, you need to know that "rightsizing" your life has positives that far outweigh the negatives. Rightsizing is about releasing the emotional attachment we have to our possessions and letting things go that no longer serve us. We are not defined by our possessions. This concept applies to our business and personal lives. Ponder this idea for much more than a moment. Create your own workable system that reflects your style of organization. The point is to create and embrace something that has order so you can use your multitasking skills effectively.

Leave Your Mothering at Home. Our problem begins when we bring motherhood into the workplace. We have to assume that everyone has a mother, so no one needs another mother coddling him or her at work. In other words, you don't need to plan all the work parties, buy all the boss's gifts, or do the jobs that men just don't want to do because they aren't naturally good at them. Don't volunteer to play the group secretary because you're better at taking notes. Such behaviors diminish your power in the workplace.

Although people may love you for your motherly contributions, they will not rally behind you and support you as their leader.

Take Risks. By taking risks, not only do we learn how to be brave but we discover opportunities that lead to fabulous outcomes. More women need to change their mind-set regarding their ability to attain membership in the highest echelon on the corporate ladder.

> **Women limit themselves because they are sometimes afraid to take stretch jobs. I know of very few men who, given a stretch opportunity, wouldn't think that they are qualified from day one.**
>
> Francis Aldrich Sevilla-Sacasa

Few people at the end of their lives think or say, "I wish I had been more conservative and taken fewer risks." The woman who goes the furthest is generally the one who is willing to take chances. Predictable "sure things" slowly nudge us toward our goals. Calculated risks, however, can take us leaps and bounds beyond the competition. Our culture encourages conservatism, yet we admire those who are brave enough to take the road less traveled. Remember that calculated risks do not involve reckless abandon. They are based on experience, knowledge, and a certain amount of due diligence.

Taking Credit

Show the world what you can do and hold on to the credit. Women too often divert attention away from themselves because they aren't familiar with the limelight. It is more natural for women to say, "Oh, it's no big deal" or "It was a team effort." This attitude keeps potentially *great* women at just good and gives less-capable competitors an open invitation to pass them by.

Make Yourself Known. Find ways to impress high-level people. Seek them out at company meetings and chat with them in the elevator. Use every opportunity to give great answers to simple questions. For example, "How are you?" could be answered with "I am really committed to our team and love working on the X project. I'm seeing great results." Relying only on your immediate boss to get ahead is a strategy for low-level employees. Self-promotion is not boastful. It is smart!

> By taking risks, not only do we learn how to be brave but we discover opportunities that lead to fabulous outcomes.

For example, Benet was encouraged by her mentor to speak up about her accomplishments instead of assuming she would be appropriately recognized for her efforts. Her boss assumed that she was happy in her current role because it fit her lifestyle, which included her two children and spouse. Instead, he groomed the "whippersnappers," who were young, single, and male. He was surprised when Benet told him that her husband performed the role of caretaker for their children and was a stay-at-home dad so that her own career could escalate. Her boss had made assumptions in the absence of facts because she had not taken the time to act in her own best interests.

Speak up and be heard. Even though an outside champion is a wonderful advocate, a self-champion is required to get ahead.

Remember That It Is Easier to Beg for Forgiveness Than to Ask for Permission. I once worked for a nice man who always looked out for himself. A new division of the company had opened and I desperately wanted to join that team, but I was my boss's best performer. I met all the tenure and performance criteria and was the obvious choice for the new job. The people at corporate headquarters even sent me a personal message saying that they automatically thought of me for the team. However, my boss was less than excited about this proposition and used reverse psychology to show me how good I actually had it. He also played on my female martyr tendencies and told me how much he and the team needed me. He finally agreed to speak to "the powers that be" on my behalf. The company had a strict protocol, so I had to wait until approval came.

Three weeks later my request for transfer was denied. I was told that the timing was wrong but next year it would happen. I was perplexed. The qualifications were clearly defined and I had met all of them. I sent a coy, very well-crafted e-mail to the new department. It is always better to be coy than to be direct when you are going around your boss. That way you have the option of begging for forgiveness later. My e-mail simply stated how sorry I was that I wasn't going to be part of the new team and how I regretted the outcome. I wished the team members the best of luck and shared a new idea I had for their consideration.

That was all it took. Corporate took the matter to the top and inquired as to why I wasn't being given a chance. Since there was no ethical reason for me to be denied, I got the job. When my boss asked why I had talked to corporate, I sweetly said, "I was just following up just like you always taught me. I'm so sorry if I caused any problems." The idea that it's easier to beg for forgiveness than to ask for permission is a tough concept for many women to embrace, but doing so is the best way to get ahead.

Delegate. If you want to climb the corporate ladder, you must delegate. Because women know they can "do it all," they often fall into this career-damaging trap. Delegation actually encompasses all of the three Cs since you need to have *confidence* in your leadership ability, a willingness to give and share *credit*, and *comfort* with your ability to hire, manage, and elevate those around you. One of my favorite managers would always remind me to "inspect what you expect." People make decisions based upon their relationships versus their circumstances. If you trust and respect the people you interact with, your decisions will be emotionally based. Building trust and earning respect is best done through delegation. This lets people know that you believe in their ability to get the job done. If we do everything ourselves, we deplete the quality of energy that we need to inspire people to take our lead.

Comfort with Success

You've gained some ground, so get comfortable with it. This is when women need to use their intuition and keep their enemies close. There are no coincidences in this world—everything happens for a reason. You are supposed to be in a position of power, so enjoy it. Wear it with ease and comfort like your favorite pajamas. And most importantly, think about your next promotion. That will always keep you in the game.

Act Like a Woman. Once you earn kudos in the workplace, the rules begin to shift. Women often desire key roles in companies, but they convince themselves that the sacrifices are too great. First of all, they think that in order to take a seat at the top, they need to act like a man. This is simply not true.

Men manage all people the same way and tend to leave out the personal aspects. Loyalty is best built by connecting with individuals on a personal level. Everyone must feel valued and important. People stay at or leave companies because of people. If your employees feel that you genuinely care about them, you won't find any harder workers than them. Women can easily and naturally express their caring side.

At one point in my career, I reported to a man I nicknamed "Napoleon" who was the COO of the organization. My goal was to work professionally and effectively with him within the workplace. However, he made this impossible as he demanded after-work meetings with all of the employees over several cocktails almost every evening. I also received daily complaints about his sexual innuendos and inappropriate behavior. I decided to give him enough rope to hang himself.

One day, he inquired how he could get to know the heart of the organization. I suggested that he attend various staff meetings to listen and participate. As fate would have it, he chose to attend the customer service meeting run by the most conservative woman in our company. The objective for her meeting was team building, so each individual on this all-women team was asked to share one thing she would change about her physical appearance—a very sensitive topic for women.

Following a very emotional hour of female bonding, it was Napoleon's turn to play the game. He loudly and proudly joked about the size of his "package." As he robustly laughed alone, we wrapped up the meeting. After receiving fifteen emotionally charged letters, the CEO was forced to reprimand the boorish COO—who didn't understand why the women were so upset— and his bad behavior ceased.

Men tend to leave out the details, the extra descriptions that ensure the best results. Men will often say, "They can figure it out themselves; just give them the big picture." However, many people learn best practices by being specifically told how to approach a situation. Women often confuse being detailed with being controlling, but by emulating men, we ignore one of our greatest strengths: the ability to remember all the "little things."

Many men in positions of authority are ruled by their egos and think they should be catered to. They stand in one place at company functions and expect others to approach them. When men behave this way, they are seen as powerful; however, women who act similarly are seen as cold and selfish. The art of professional mingling will set you apart. Never stay too late, never overconsume, and never get too personal.

Build Loyalty. If you work for a large company, make your team a close-bonded group within the organization. If you own your own company, create an "us against the competition" mentality. A woman works best with a strong foundation of loyal supporters to watch her back.

How do you create loyalty? Tell people what you expect and then stand behind them. Staunchly defend your people; never let anyone criticize them—except you, when you give constructive feedback. Always take responsibility for their actions. Tell them that if they do their best job, you will support them in any and all outcomes, and then do what you say. Express that you will always help them grow so they can achieve their goals, and make sure you know what those goals are for each individual.

Make certain you communicate the big picture to your team in confidence. If they can handle it, tell them more than other teams may know. This will build lasting trust. Get to know your people personally—not too personally but just enough. This is a great way to create team loyalty. People are loyal to those they believe will stay at the top because of their smarts and their integrity.

Another way to build loyalty with your superiors, peers, and employees is through giving and receiving feedback. Always acknowledge that honest feedback is difficult to both give and receive, and avoid personal attacks and defensive reactions.

When *giving* feedback, focus on behavior versus attitude and personality, and connect behavior to results. Relate and share only those situations that you have witnessed yourself; never fall victim to hearsay and unsupported accusations. Finally, when providing constructive feedback, always focus on what the person is doing *right*, not what's *wrong*.

When *receiving* feedback, be cognizant that you are not being attacked. You are being asked to engage in a thoughtful debate about your contributions. Listen and concentrate on the feedback being shared so you can provide intelligent and thoughtful rebuttals. If you receive only positive feedback, express humility and inquire if any areas could be improved upon. If you receive only negative feedback, genuinely express your desire to improve, and also ask about areas where you have displayed strength.

Display Conscious Competence and Conscious Incompetence. One of the keys to creating respected and lasting leadership is to display conscious competence and conscious incompetence. In other words, you know what you know, you know what you don't know, and you're confident enough to admit both. Hire people smarter than you so your weakest link is far superior to most teams' best players. People love to be valued for what they bring to the table. Make requests like "Educate me on how you do this" or "Help me understand the basics because I know you're the expert."

Lead by example. The highest form of flattery is imitation, so be sure that your actions are ones that you would want duplicated. Never ask others to do what you yourself have not done or would not do. People want to be led by kind, honest, strong, capable individuals who walk their walk and talk their talk, for this is a sign of immeasurable strength, knowledge, and comfort.

Keep Your Enemies Close. This lesson from Sun Tzu is testosterone based but should be heeded by successful women. If you are a dynamic leader, you will become a target to be overthrown. However, if you command loyalty and display conscious incompetence, your advocates will warn you in plenty of time for you to put on your armor. Use your intuition to figure out who feels threatened by you. Then take those people to lunch alone and get to know them better. Build consensus with them on any points that you can agree on. Where you disagree, compliment them on their stance, but don't be afraid to impress them with your courage to stand alone. Strength deters predators. If appropriate, tell an adversary that you feel you two should form an alliance so you are on the same team.

This whole process may be painful, but you will thank yourself later. Your rivals are insecure people who need someone to attack, so you must deflect their attention away from you. It is much easier to avoid an attack altogether than to waste precious time killing a predator.

Be aware that enemies can appear in the form of bullies, gossips, and backstabbers. They are similar yet different. Watch all of them carefully. They are intimidated by your power and may want to eliminate you, hoping that this will make room for them.

Bullies must be confronted head on. They are insecure and are misguided in believing that a "tough stance" equates to capability and respect. Be diplomatic and professional but very direct. Make statements like "I will not be bullied and I will not be intimidated. We are going to have to find a way to work this out or you are going to have to find another target to pick on." Always end your conversation with a bully by stating your professional intention: "I am here to do my job; I am confident in my abilities and know what needs to be done, so I plan to do that with or without your support and endorsement. You can work against me or with me."

If you are ever confronted by a bully in a group setting, never lower yourself to his or her standards in petty behavior. Always make a strong statement that lets the observers know that you plan to address the issue. "It is inappropriate to have this discussion at this time and I don't appreciate your tone, so let's discuss this offline following the meeting."

If women are gossiping behind your back, rise above it. Consider it their own problem. If it continues, you need to directly address it in a professional manner behind closed doors. This is when diplomacy will put any issues to rest. Say something like, "I'm not sure what I may have done to upset you, but I have worked very hard to get to where I am, and I hope that we can agree to disagree and work collaboratively together. I would always speak to you directly about any issues I may have with you, and I hope in the future you will do the same."

The most dangerous backstabbers are those who have equal authority with you because they can sway the opinions of your superiors. Do not engage in negative verbal banter with a backstabber, but always address the accusations so *your* superiors know your perspective. People are not mind readers, so you need to always proactively represent yourself. Make an effort to nip all potential problems in the bud, and if you even suspect that there is a potential problem, check to be sure: "Hi, I'm just stopping by to make sure we're on the same page" or "I know we always have clear communication, but it never hurts to double-check." Passive behavior is based on the hope that an enemy will go away; this is denial. It assumes that all parties involved will dismiss the backstabber and realize the truth on their own and release you from blame. Instead, use diplomacy and "straight talk" to address issues head on and negate the power and impact of backstabbers.

Play Politics. Simply put, politics is building relationships. Everyone knows that the best way to get something done is to influence people you know. If you get an endorsement from someone who is "connected," people will embrace hiring you, promoting you, or rallying behind you. Every corporate environment in America, large or small, has some level of political game playing. If you spend time getting to know the players, you will never get caught in the political cross fire. Think of politics as self-promotion. Let people know who you are and what you stand for in a way that is in alliance with them. Politics is also about the spin you put on what you want.

The three key components of successful office politics are negotiation, communication, and persuasion. These are all related to the power of the spoken word. According to Brizendine, "Girls use language to get consensus, influencing others without telling them directly what to do . . . Boys use language to command others, get things done, brag, threaten, ignore a partner's suggestion, and override each other's attempts to speak."[6] This difference gives women the competitive edge in politics.

Any good campaign manager will tell you that you start running for the next term on the day you get into office. If you network, make acquaintances, and build rapport, you will never have to worry about company politics. Men commonly build rapport only with people they personally like and have things in common with. This way of thinking is corporate suicide. Get to know as many people as possible by setting up lunch meetings and thirty-minute "how can we work together?" sessions. Always preface your meetings with your intention to work better together.

Treat Everyone as an Individual. When it comes to management, nothing is worse than the equal treatment of unequals! Many women in business make this huge mistake. We focus on everyone playing nicely together and being as fair as we can possibly be, when instead we need to constantly recruit the best players. Each player on a team brings a different value to the table, and each should be treated accordingly. When leaders employ this strategy, they catapult their power to uncapped heights.

Here's an example. I took a job with a pharmaceutical company that was hemorrhaging money—$9 million a quarter to be exact. My healthy ego convinced me that I could be Florence Nightingale, so I jumped in over my head. I knew I had nothing to lose and everything to gain. I immediately conducted an assessment of the problems. I quickly discovered that the corporate culture was chauvinistic and driven by fear and intimidation. The corporate bible was *What Would Machiavelli Do? The Ends Justify the Meanness.* In desperation the owner had stepped in as CEO, and he was more than willing to embrace any and all of my suggestions to save his company.

In order for me to save the dying planet, one major obstacle had to fall: a man I fondly called "Boss Hog." He had all the makings of a true "redneck" and had a position of authority equal to mine. He didn't require the male sales representatives to work in the office more than one day a week. The females were required to work in the office five days a week because he figured they were cutting corners anyway because they also had to be housewives. He directed his salesmen to take physicians to topless bars because that was how to get their business. This directive was actually shared in corporate memos and distributed across the country. His management team was composed of sexist henchmen who hired any male candidate who applied or provocatively dressed, insecure women who believed in sleeping their way to the top. The incentive plan consisted of bonuses allocated based on the managers' subjective opinions. Working hard was never a consideration, but schmoozing with the right people was absolutely required.

The larger problem was that the owner was a terrible judge of character. I realized that he judged people on how well they catered to his ego, so I simply played by the rules of the game. I prepared a heartfelt speech as to why I should have full authority to reorganize the company. Boss Hog was doing what he had always done, and the results were horrible. Dramatic and swift change was required.

The professional demise of Boss Hog brought considerable uproar, including death threats and the resignation of several henchmen. Since the top performers were treated no better and no worse than the bottom performers, women had been treated as second-class citizens, and the administrative staff members had been considered slaves, I became "the people's champ."

Be Flexible. To get and keep the cream of the crop, today's best leaders are flexible about the way people work. Some people need a traditional work environment to succeed, others excel within a virtual environment, and some flextimers give 150 percent because they are so grateful to have a position that works for them. Many male leaders are more traditional when it comes to corporate environments because they need control to feel power. They gain control by creating workplaces where people are judged on how early they come in, how late they stay, and how often they play politics with the boss. This corporate mentality sends a message that as long as you are physically in the office, you're assumed to be working. This weak leadership may get you foot soldiers, but in today's world, the quality generals—those who can help you carry your load—want to be managed individually, not based on a norm.

I once interviewed a very qualified female candidate for a high-profile, director-level position. Near the conclusion of our interview, her compelling request for flextime hours began: "I will give you 150 percent of my effort, but two days a week, I must leave at 2 p.m. for my childcare commitment. Once my children are asleep, I will finish my projects for the day at home, and our goals will always be met without skipping a beat." Much to the dismay of my immediate supervisor, I hired her. It was one of the best hiring decisions I ever made in my career. She outperformed, overcommitted, and exceeded every expectation. She was staunchly loyal to me and went out of her way to go "above and beyond" whenever possible.

According to a 2006 report, "inflexible, all-or-nothing workplaces drive women—and men—into neo-traditional roles. . . . The result is many fathers working longer hours than they would like and many mothers working fewer hours than they would like."[7] An article that appeared in *The Economist* stated that "greater participation by women in the labour market could help to offset the effects of an ageing, shrinking population and hence support growth."[8] In addition, it was noted that "employed moms spend 82 percent as much time on childcare activities as do non-employed moms."[9]

If corporations would take the needs of working women seriously, this would strengthen not only our economy but also our family values. It is difficult to accept that our progressive nation can't make the appropriate adjustments to allow women to be both corporate players and engaged mothers. If raising our next generation were truly a top priority, we should want women, who play the key roles of advisor and nurturer, to be as happy as possible. If it were easier to combine bottles and briefcases, more families and more companies would receive quality contributions from women. If women were allowed to have it all—motherhood and a fulfilling career—everyone would benefit. In the 1980s, Marilyn Waring was the first economist to consider the impact of unpaid house-work. She concluded that if counted economically, "women's work" would constitute the world's single largest service and pro-duction sector.[10]

You will get the very best from your people by working with their unique situations when you can. A basic formal structure should always be in place, but a willingness to be pliable regard-ing agreed-upon terms will pay the best dividends. Women espe-cially will do more if you empathize with their needs. And all people become more committed and invested in a relationship based on a partnership, not a dictatorship. Remember that victims see problems, flatliners see solutions, and deliberate creators see possibilities.

Also remember to be flexible with yourself. When asked, "What do you think about the need for balance?" Carol Bartz, exec-utive chairman of Autodesk Inc., replied, "The problem with bal-ance is it denotes perfection. And you can't do that. Balance is waking up at 4:30 a.m. and getting your exercise in . . . And mak-ing sure you get a hot breakfast ready to go and your kids are ready for school and then putting your kitchen back in order . . . You do a great job at work. And along the way, you also do a little charity work and make sure to reach out to friends because we have to stay in touch and get that Rolodex going."[11]

Comfort is creating your own definition of balance that you can stand behind, defend, and never make excuses for. It is find-ing security in standing alone. It is fearlessness in choosing the road less traveled. Standing alone not only builds character but also is a testimony to being comfortable in your own skin. When you have the willingness to be wrong alone and the confidence to be right without gloating, you've reached the point of ultimate comfort.

Never Confuse Motion with Action

In this life there are no coincidences. Everything happens for a reason. You were supposed to read this book, whether you received it as a gift, you heard about it from a friend, or you just happened upon it by chance. It is now your responsibility to extract from the pages anything that will add value to your life and help you saddle up your own white horse. It is also your responsibility to extract the value each message can provide to other women so that, in the spirit of a cavalry, you can help them saddle up their white horses as well.

Change Your Attitude

The first step is to take a nonresistant attitude toward existing conditions. What does this mean? Who you are is not who you were when you started reading this book—it is who you will choose to be as a result of reading it. Don't judge or place blame on yourself for being in a situation that is less than desirable. Instead, seek the truth and agree with it. Accept that your decisions have led you to an undesirable place, find the confidence to know that your situation is temporary, and call on the courage to make a change. If having what we wanted were easy, the world would be filled with deliberate creators. If it weren't possible, only victims and flatliners would exist. The power of self-control is that we have a choice every day to live intentionally. And the only person we can control is ourselves.

> **The greatest lesson of my life: to recognize that I am solely responsible for it.**
>
> *Oprah Winfrey*

We might like to control our husbands, our children, or our coworkers, but the reality is that once we control our own actions by aligning them with our core values, all the actions of others will naturally seem to be in line with our own. We must look at life as a game of inches and know that those inches can lead to miles of progress. Remember: it is not the world outside you that dictates your circumstances, it is the world inside of you. Your attitude really is everything.

You can change your thought process in moments simply by adjusting your attitude, the positive or negative thoughts you embrace. Victims focus on the past and what they don't have. Deliberate creators focus on the present, where they can have an impact, and they never confuse motion with action. To become one of them, you need to take the deliberate step to spend time on only what you can change because nothing else matters. Realize that the power of your thoughts is so great that you can eliminate all opposing factors that may be obstacles to your success.

The current focus in self-help is cognitive behavioral therapy. This technique concentrates on fixing the present. People learn that their negative thoughts about themselves are distorted, and they learn to live in the present. Don't waste time judging yourself for your past missteps; encourage yourself to make new steps in the right direction and set daily attainable goals to get where you want to be. Use your multitasking skills to your advantage, and use your intuition to end alliances with people, groups, hobbies, and tasks that drain your energy and add no value.

The following story demonstrates the power of our thoughts and just how much control we actually have over our own destiny.

After one gynecological exam, I was told I had a "closed cervix" and that my chances of becoming pregnant were very slim. Although several doctors surmised that this condition was the result of an earlier trauma, one fabulous physician plainly said to me, "There is no clinical reason that your cervix should be closed; maybe it's psychological."

Until I was thirty-six years old, I didn't hear my biological clock ticking. I had been the willing caregiver to every person in my life. I actually took pride in providing guidance to strangers, acquaintances, friends, and family and felt that this responsibility was enough for my lifetime. I genuinely felt that I was on my chosen path and had no unmet need for motherhood. In fact, I felt relieved to be in a society that didn't ostracize women if they chose not to have children.

One day my mother reminded me of an interview that I had given five years earlier. I was asked, "Will there ever be a time in your life when you would like to have a child?"

My answer was an emphatic yes but with very specific conditions. I needed to be in a personal and professional space where I was living my passion, which is empowering women to be all they can be. This meant speaking, coaching, teaching, and writing about the subtle inequalities that still exist today. This also meant persuading women to give themselves permission to put themselves first, knowing that it is the least selfish thing they can do for others.

In September 2006, I realized that all my conditions had been met, so I made a grand proposition to my husband: "If I'm meant to get pregnant, it will happen effortlessly and quickly, so let's try once while I'm ovulating. If it is meant to be, it will be so." My husband, who is an expert at humoring me, agreed to what he secretly thought was a preposterous idea. And since it involved sex, he was perfectly happy to go along with my plan.

My life continued at its normal, hectic pace, and I forgot all about my little experiment. However, three months later, when I had tender breasts, an expanded waistline, and a craving for oranges, it suddenly hit me that I might be pregnant. I happened to be in a pharmacy buying hair color when I had this epiphany, so I purchased a pregnancy test, which I administered in the pharmacy bathroom. To my complete shock, the test was positive. I promptly purchased six more tests, ran to my car, and hyperventilated all the way home. Certain my first test was defective, I immediately took the six remaining tests. I called my husband and said, "You must come home immediately!" When he finally was able to accept that I really was pregnant, we both recognized that the power of intention is an extraordinary gift, and when directed positively, it can manifest miracles.

Whether we put the truth first or second makes all the difference in the world. Often, we know the truth deep within ourselves and understand exactly what needs to be done to remedy a given situation but decide that denial is an easier pill to swallow. Choice is the most underrated option we have as women. By limiting our choices, we agree to settle for less and live a life of denial. The worst part about denial is that we consciously choose to hit the "hold button" on our own lives. Temporary detours and bumps in the road can sometimes provide a needed wake-up call to initiate change in our lives. They can make us realize that times have been better and that our situation has the potential to be good again.

These moments give us the opportunity to transition from victims and flatliners to deliberate creators.

> **I've learned from experience that the greater part of our happiness or misery comes from our dispositions and not our circumstances.**
>
> *Martha Washington*

Let's look at a common scenario of denial. You're in a relationship that you know is not going anywhere because you've outgrown it. You want it to end, but that would require moving out, breaking someone's heart, divorce, or all of the above. You wait and hope that the other person will end the relationship. Deep down, you know that it is not a probable scenario, yet you bide your time and pray for a miracle. As you tread water, your self-worth diminishes. As an avoidance tactic, you capitalize on any opportunity to work late or be with friends so your denial is more tolerable. Your inner martyr justifies your behavior by reminding you of all the good parts of your relationship that other people would die for. You are a flatliner. You keep reminding yourself of all the worse relationships you could be in. You wonder if maybe you are taking a "great" relationship for granted. If you are controlled by your ego, you will tell yourself that you are noble for maintaining the relationship because your partner would be crushed if you left him.

In reality, it is selfish to assume that someone wouldn't be happier in a relationship that actually involved reciprocated affection. Putting yourself first includes having the courage to be alone.

Wake-up calls can have varying levels, and what may be mild to you could be severe to someone else. For example, a mild wake-up call may come the moment you see 500 wedding photos posted on a Web site for the world to view and realize you are the plump bridesmaid in 350 selections. Sometimes it takes more than looking in the mirror every day to decide to take care of what you can control, what you feed your body. Our ability to hear a wake-up call depends on our judgment of ourselves, not the judgment of others, and on what we are willing to settle for. Denial can easily become motivation if we can embrace the idea of possibility thinking. Your physical appearance is your way of showing the outside world what your inside looks like.

We should strive to be comfortable in our own skin and be willing to refute our own denial. The best example I have of this concept is a response I received to my blog entry entitled "Empowered Woman: Pussycat Doll or Call Girl?" I had commented on the tag line used to promote the Pussycat Dolls reality show that implied that a Pussycat Doll was an empowered woman. A reader responded: "As a fat girl . . . I hate the Pussycat Dolls for obvious reasons. Part of me says it's just another example of the media shoving down our throats that you can't get a date if you're not a size 2. You want to really empower women? Show them how to use their minds and not just shake their behinds. Place more emphasis on self-development than breast development. The other part of me, the more quiet part, is still somewhat jealous that I can't prance around on some stage somewhere, in some tiny little outfit, and get paid to do it. It's a conflict of interest, isn't it?"[1] She impressed me with her balance between self-deprecation and a genuine desire to be her "best self." Consciously recognizing denial is the first step in making changes and eliminating the excuses that keep us from achieving our goals.

Major denial may come when you see signs that your body can't keep up with your desires. This doesn't happen only at retirement age. Many thirty- and forty-year-olds experience the harsh reality that without proper use and conditioning, the body can't perform well on demand. In all cases, the wake-up call to make adjustments is hard. Some women take this realization much harder than others, especially when the necessary changes require new eating, drinking, and exercise habits. An adjustment may be as simple as reducing a three-times-weekly cocktail schedule to once a week. Perhaps creating a scheduled exercise routine is the best way to achieve results. Regardless of the problem, accepting that one exists and that you need to take action to embrace your wake-up call is the most important step in shifting away from denial.

Remember that life is a game of inches. If you suddenly make dramatic adjustments you probably will not maintain them for the long term, so be realistic and reasonable in your expectations. Set SMART goals. An example of an unrealistic goal is a pregnant woman's plan to leave the hospital wearing the jeans she fit into nine months ago. When I hear a woman make this kind of goal, I immediately size her up for a straightjacket because it's lunacy to expect to be sexy a day after giving birth.

Finally, let me mention two common forms of denial: escapism and extremism. I define "escapism" as the "habitual diversion of the mind to purely imaginative activity or a hiatus from reality or routine." The logical part of you knows that you won't just happen upon the life you want to live; you need to create it. Escapism, however, allows you to wander around in a "subconscious fog" where everything is fine. You're living in a dream world. Whereas victims believe their own excuses for accepting a less-than-happy life, escapists don't even make excuses because they are pretending that life is bliss.

My definition of "extremism" is "behavior that exemplifies measures beyond the norm." Overeating, undereating, overdrinking, overspending, promiscuity, overworking, and overexercise are all examples of extremism. We mask our pain with excessive behavior and simply create more of the pain we are trying to avoid. Supersizing is too much of a good thing. If you don't believe me, watch the movie *Super Size Me*. And I'm sure you've heard the old sayings

"Don't bite off more than you can chew" and "Your eyes are bigger than your belly." Our mothers and grandmothers tried to teach us the dangers of excess, but for some those lessons fell on deaf ears.

Inside Looking Out

Embrace the fact that nothing in life has meaning until you give it meaning. You're the one who decides to accept or reject any positive or negative thoughts or comments from others. Putting yourself first means making a conscious and deliberate decision to be impenetrable to negativity. It means understanding the impact of negative words, thoughts, and actions and deliberately choosing to create positive energy in all your interactions. Prosperity doesn't happen by accident; it is the result of sincere intention. Likewise, success doesn't happen by accident; it is the result of following the universal laws of nature that were discussed in principle 1—the laws that all deliberate creators know.

Remember: a person's greatest emotional need is to be appreciated, to be significant. It is your responsibility to appreciate yourself so you can truly appreciate others.

Don't undermine your self-worth by comparing yourself to others. The quirky, individual characteristics in each of us make us memorable and special. We never admire others for being the same. We admire the square pegs that refuse to fit into round holes.

Measure your contributions by the weight of their impact on you and everybody you have the ability to influence. Always set your goals according to what *you* deem important. Only *you* know what is best for your own life. Be open to learning new things because knowledge can never be taken away and can only be strengthened.

Provide attentive care for yourself. Identify the areas of your life where you would like to see improvement and identify new knowledge that you would like to obtain. Seek out seminars, courses, and networking groups where you can gain this knowledge and make a commitment to yourself to spend as much time on character building as you do on outward aesthetics. Manicures, pedicures, and massages are wonderful, and you should have more of them, but are they making a deposit toward your "inner growth"? The more we invest in building our self-worth inwardly and outwardly, the more we will have to draw from when others need our broad shoulders and thick skin.

Take the time you need to reflect, gain clarity, and care for yourself. Maybe it's an hour a day or an hour and a half every other day or even thirty minutes, but "you" time must be planned. You know that others are depending upon you; you must recharge your batteries so you too can rely upon yourself.

Finally, remember these truths:

- Putting yourself first is the least selfish thing you can do for others.
- Never confuse motion with action.
- Seek the truth and agree with it.
- Your thoughts become your actions.
- Two things that can never be retrieved are words and time.
- People treat you the way you allow yourself to be treated.
- The universe is designed with no limitations; the only ceiling that exists is the one you create.

> **Far away there in the sunshine are my highest aspirations. I may not reach them, but I can look up and see their beauty, believe in them, and try to follow where they lead.**
>
> *Louisa May Alcott*

A Woman's Declaration

In this time of evolution, advancement, and progression, unite in purpose with the women of the world to redirect our efforts toward putting ourselves first so that we may have more to give back to others. Instead of focusing on how far we still have to go to achieve equality, we will simply step into our rightful place as the leaders in our relationships.

We will use our emotional intelligence and our intuition not only for sensing what is not working in our lives but for sensing what is working and acknowledge that and notice what needs to be done in our sphere of influence to raise others' consciousness. We will use our natural diplomacy to say all the uncomfortable things that must be said in order for injustice to be minimized.

We will live our daily lives with the knowledge that we are building not only our own runway but a platform for those who will follow us. Our stamp of authorship will be significant because we are here to make a difference, and though that difference may start and stop within our own circle, those inches will lead to miles of progress.

By recognizing and accepting our own individual power, we do not overshadow others but instead lift them up to strive for their maximum potential. We will make apparent to the naked eye the infinite possibilities that truly exist. The responsibility to shine our brightest light is an urgent one that we will embrace now.

We will take a nonresistant attitude toward existing conditions and know that who we are is who we decide to be today, in this moment. We will not judge or praise our past missteps or successes for we understand that we are a result of our experiences and this understanding will fuel our passion.

We agree to set our intention for each day with the knowledge that prosperity in every aspect of our life is attainable. We are ready to claim it by acknowledging our gifts of intuition, multitasking, and emotional intelligence.

We will stand and be counted and inspire other women to step up and embrace their power so no woman will be invisible but instead be invincible.

I will personally add my heart, my thoughts, and my actions and join in this coalition for women.

I proclaim my daily commitment to put myself first, knowing that it is the least selfish thing I can do for others.

_____   _____

Signed   _Date_

Resources

Whether you're interested in learning more about pregnancy and motherhood, women's empowerment, healthy living, or your career, you'll find helpful books, Web sites, and organizations in this section.

Recommended Books

Healthy Living

John Robbins, *Diet for a New America: How Your Food Choices Affect Your Life, Happiness, and the Future of Life on Earth*, 2nd ed. (Tiburon, CA: H. J. Kramer, 1998)

The son of one of the founders of the ice cream giant Baskin-Robbins shares shocking and powerful facts about the food we put into our bodies. This book should be read by anyone concerned about a healthy lifestyle.

David Wolfe, *Eating for Beauty: For Women and Men—Introducing a Whole New Concept of Beauty, What It Is and How You Can Achieve It* (San Diego, CA: Maul Brothers, 2003)

Proper nutrition can have an impact on your outside as well as your inside. This book outlines the many benefits that beautifying foods can have on your life.

Linda Page, ND, PhD, *Healthy Healing: A Guide to Self-Healing for Everyone*, 12th ed. (Carmel Valley, CA: Healthy Healing Publications, 2004)
Everything you need to know to be your own herbal pharmacist is included in this robust guide. Ailments, health conditions, lifestyle choices, and detoxification are all plainly and thoroughly examined and explained.

F. Batmanghelidj, MD, *Water for Health, for Healing, for Life: You're Not Sick, You're Thirsty!* (New York: Warner Books, 2003)
Twenty years of clinical and scientific research are shared in this book, which concludes that water may be the answer to a majority of our medical conditions. You will never take the power of hydration lightly again.

Ann Wigmore, *The Wheatgrass Book: How to Grow and Use Wheatgrass to Maximize Your Health and Vitality* (New York: Avery, 1985)
The amazing benefits of the health elixir wheatgrass are shared in this simple, how-to guide to growing wheatgrass and using it to improve your life.

General Favorites

Robert Fulghum, *All I Really Need to Know I Learned in Kindergarten* (New York: Ballantine, 2003)
This is a light, refreshing compilation of common-sense stories and practical wisdom.

Frank Warren, *PostSecret: Extraordinary Confessions from Ordinary Lives* (New York: Regan Books, 2005)
Ever wish you had someone to tell your secrets to? Fill out a post-card and send it away. This is exactly what Frank Warren encourages in his provocative collection of anonymous confessions.

Gary Goldschneider and Joost Elffers, *The Secret Language of Birthdays: Your Complete Personology Guide for Each Day of the Year* (New York: Studio, 2003)
Individual profiles are given for every day of the year. Each profile offers advice and a usually accurate view of who you are based on the day you were born, including your strengths and weaknesses.

Annie Leibovitz and Susan Sontag, *Women* (New York: Random House, 1999)
This is a coffee table book filled with extraordinary photographs of extraordinary women.

Pregnancy and Motherhood

Vicki Iovine, *The Girlfriends' Guide to Pregnancy* (New York: Pocket Books, 2007)
The author presents a candid, humorous look at pregnancy and motherhood. This book is a realistic view of the joys, trials, and tribulations of becoming a mother.

Peter Tallack, *In the Womb: Witness the Journey from Conception to Birth through Astonishing 3D Images* (Washington, DC: National Geographic Society, 2006)
This is a perfect pregnancy book for couples. The photography is amazing, and the simple, concise descriptions of child development engage both parents in the gestation process. I constantly referred to this book throughout my pregnancy.

Judith Warner, *Perfect Madness: Motherhood in the Age of Anxiety* (New York: Berkley Publishing Group, 2006)
A clever, highly astute view of the mania surrounding motherhood. This book will jolt and delight you and dispel society's myths about "mothering."

Laura Walther Nathanson, MD, FAAP, *The Portable Pediatrician: A Practicing Pediatrician's Guide to Your Child's Growth, Development, Health and Behavior, from Birth to Age Five* (New York: Harper-Collins, 2002)
This book provides answers to all your health questions, both simple and complex.

Women's Empowerment

Gail Collins, *America's Women: 400 Years of Dolls, Drudges, Helpmates, and Heroines* (New York: Harper Perennial, 2007)
This history covers more than four centuries and shares stories about the women who helped shape our nation and create a place for women in America.

Catherine Ponder, *The Dynamic Laws of Prosperity* (Marina del Rey, CA: DeVorss Publications, 1985)
Of all Ponder's books, this one is my favorite because it teaches that prosperity is more than having money in the bank. Not meant to be read in one sitting, the book is divided into sections so you can explore topics that interest you at different points in your life.

Louann Brizendine, MD, *The Female Brain* (New York: Broadway, 2006)
The fundamental and clinical differences between the male brain and the female brain are described in this intriguing book. The

facts are both fascinating and empowering because they show that the female brain is truly the superior brain.

Florence Scovel Shinn, *The Game of Life for Women: And How to Play It* (Marina del Rey, CA: DeVorss & Company, 2003)
This hard-hitting book of only eighty-seven pages covers the game of life. It examines the basic laws of nature and provides practical guidance and a wake-up call for women.

Dawna Markova, *I Will Not Die an Unlived Life: Reclaiming Purpose and Passion* (Berkeley, CA: Conari Press, 2000)
This book focuses on helping you find out who you really are and how to heal what is broken within you. Anyone in search of a transformation or a new view of the future should read this.

Dr. Patti Feuereisen and Caroline Pincus, *Invisible Girls: The Truth about Sexual Abuse—A Book for Teen Girls, Young Women, and Everyone Who Cares about Them* (Emeryville, CA: Seal Press, 2005)
Powerful stories and encouraging messages about sexual abuse are presented. Targeted at teen girls and young women, this book tells unspoken truths about the silent torture that exists among abuse victims and encourages women to rise above their pain and to persevere.

Robin Morgan, *Sisterhood Is Forever: The Women's Anthology for a New Millennium* (New York: Washington Square Press, 2003)
This is a compilation of sixty original essays from feminist leaders and activists. The topics include women's healthcare, politics, spirituality, sexual preferences, and more.

Robin Morgan, *Sisterhood Is Global: The International Women's Movement Anthology* (New York: Feminist Press, 1996)

This anthology is made up of essays by women, famous or otherwise, from over seventy countries, including politicians, scholars, and journalists. The essays focus on the diversity and similarity of women's experiences throughout the world.

Lisa Grunwald and Stephen J. Adler, eds., *Women's Letters: America from the Revolutionary War to the Present* (New York: Dial Press, 2005) Four hundred letters written by amazing women over the last three centuries provide an intimate insight into the life of each woman and show her role in shaping the events we read about today.

Recommended Web Sites

Healthy Living

The Mayo Clinic
http://www.mayoclinic.com
There are an overwhelming number of health and medical sites to choose from. The Mayo Clinic provides a one-stop resource center for all kinds of reliable health information.

Medline Plus
http://medlineplus.gov/
You'll find numerous resources from the U.S. National Library of Medicine and the National Institutes of Health, including a medical encyclopedia and dictionary, current health news, information on over seven hundred health topics, and a huge section on women's health issues.

The National Women's Health Information Center
http://womenshealth.gov/

This site is a service of the Office on Women's Health in the U.S. Department of Health and Human Services. It offers current information on more than eight hundred topics pertaining to women's health today.

Organic Foodee
http://www.organicfoodee.com
This online organic food magazine will teach you everything you need to know about organic living, including recipes, herbal remedies, shopping, and the best food choices for you and your family.

Running Map
http://www.runningmap.com
Ever wonder how far that morning jog actually was? This Web site allows you to track your running path anywhere you might go and determine the distance you've run.

Parenting Tools and Family Resources

Birthday in a Box
http://www.birthdayinabox.com
You will never have to leave your home to plan the best birthday party for your child. Check one more thing off your to-do list.

Discovery Education
http://www.discoveryschool.com
This site, part of the Discovery Channel family, is dedicated to making teaching and learning exciting for students, teachers, and parents. Discovery Education provides all the lesson plans, topics for discussion, objectives, and materials needed to learn or teach any subject for any age range.

iNeighbors

http://www.ineighbors.org

You never have to wonder what's happening in your neck of the woods. This site takes community to the next level by identifying activities in your own local neighborhood.

The Learning Lighthouse

http://www.thelearninglighthouse.com

Wish your child had an at-home tutor? The Learning Lighthouse is an online tutoring program in which your child can interact with a real person, ask questions, and participate in discussions on any classroom subject.

Modern Mom

http://www.modernmom.com

Modern Mom covers every topic women care about—families and parenting, a night out on the town with your spouse, financial planning, the latest trends, and more.

My Precious Kid

http://www.mypreciouskid.com

My Precious Kid provides child safety products and safe baby gear for you and your family.

RootsWeb

http://www.rootsweb.com

Ever wanted to research your family tree? RootsWeb guides you through every step of the process of discovering your ancestry.

Taskmasters

Craigslist

http://www.craigslist.com

Find a job, a ride to work, or a television to buy, or sell your car in one day. All of these things are possible on Craigslist. This free resource is available in dozens of towns across the country.

Hassle Me!
http://www.hassleme.co.uk
We all need a personal assistant to remind us of daily commitments. Hassle Me is a virtual conscience that nags you by e-mail daily, weekly, monthly, or randomly to keep you on track. The messages can range from empowering statements to medical appointments.

How Stuff Works
http://www.howstuffworks.com
How Stuff Works is a detailed look at how things actually work—everything from your cell phone to the judicial system. How Stuff Works also offers consumer opinions and ratings to help you make the best consumer choices.

Women's Empowerment

BlogHer
http://blogher.org
You'll find blogs by women arranged by topic, including business and careers, health and wellness, technology and Web, and more.

Downtown Women's Club
http://www.downtownwomensclub.com/
Get access to online and in-person networks nationwide. The site covers jobs and resources, event calendars, discounts, chat rooms, and more.

Feminist.com
http://www.feminist.com/

This online community and portal of resources and information supports women's equality, justice, wellness, and safety.

Free-Grant-Kit.com
http://www.free-grant-kit.com
Free-Grant-Kit.com allows you to access all available governmental grants on a monthly basis. Categories include women's grants, personal grants, business grants, and more.

iVillage
http://www.ivillage.com
Established in 1995, this huge site for women offers videos, blogs, shopping, online courses, social networking tools, and articles on health, parenting, beauty, fitness, food, relationships, and entertainment.

Ladies Who Launch
http://www.ladieswholaunch.com
This women-only networking group is designed to teach women about various aspects of running a business or a project. Browse resources and tips online or find an event in your area.

National Association for Female Executives
http://www.nafe.com
This thirty-five-year-old organization offers networking opportunities across the country. Publications include *Working Mother* magazine.

National Association of Women Business Owners
http://www.nawbo.org
This organization is "the voice of America's 10.6 million women-owned businesses." Find business resources, local and national events, and more.

NOW (National Organization for Women)
http://www.now.org
Founded in 1966, NOW is the largest organization of feminist activists in the United States with five hundred thousand contributing members and 550 chapters in all fifty states and the District of Columbia.

She Knows Network
http://www.sheknows.com
Browse this site for information about pregnancy and motherhood, health and fitness, style, travel, and more.

Vocation Vacations
http://www.vocationvacations.com
Test-drive your dream job while you enjoy a vacation. This site allows you to explore any career for a short period of time and determine whether or not it's a "fit" with your life.

Women's International Center
http://www.wic.org
This organization encourages women to learn, teach, and create. Check the birthdates list to be inspired by the women who share your special day.

Women's Media
http://www.womensmedia.com/
This site offers "tools for your life" for working women. Read articles about being self-employed, achieving financial success, taking care of yourself, simplifying your life, and more.

Twenty Pregnancy Tips

You can find thousands of books about pregnancy. They all contain well-meant advice (as well as some terrifying and some mundane information), but they are usually boring because many authors go on and on about minute points. In addition, you'll find little consistency in the mountains of advice.

These twenty tips cover what you really need to know. You can find a list of books I do recommend in appendix A.

1. *Choose your prenatal vitamins carefully.* All prenatal vitamins are not created equal. Do not believe a physician who tells you that you can pick any brand that makes you feel good. My humble recommendation is to "go organic." Most nonorganic vitamins contain dyes and fillers, so you are not receiving 100 percent nutrition. If you are going to follow the daily routine of taking a prenatal vitamin, you may as well take one with 100 percent benefits. New Chapter Organic Perfect Prenatal vitamins are 100 percent organic and contain no artificial flavors or colors.

2. *Fight morning sickness by staying hydrated.* Morning sickness is directly tied to dehydration. The more hydrated you are, the less morning sickness you will have. A vicious cycle ensues when dehydration exists: morning sickness starts, and not only do you

become more dehydrated, but you have a lessened desire to eat or drink anything, thus ensuring that dehydration continues. If you weren't a water drinker before your pregnancy, jump on the bandwagon now.

3. *Grease your body like a cooking pan.* Stretch marks can be hereditary, but don't let that defeat you before you have fought the battle. I recommend a daily slathering of jojoba oil. Your skin is the biggest organ of your body, so be conscious that anything you place on your skin should be safe to put in your mouth. Many moisturizers and stretch-mark solutions are filled with drying chemicals that will counteract your efforts.

4. *Pregnancy is no time for a "new do."* Let me clarify. You should look and feel as lovely as possible during pregnancy, but all the new and unfamiliar changes brought on by pregnancy motivate many women to change their hair styles. Often, our hair is the only thing we can actually control about our appearance during pregnancy. But 99.9 percent of the time, you will regret a dramatic style change. Every pregnant woman I have met has confirmed this statement. Hair coloring is another issue. I am not a fan of dark roots, but my conscience would not allow me to use a chemical dye in the name of beauty. Please be assured that vegetable dye alternatives are available at your local natural food store that will pacify you for nine months.

5. *Fight constipation with wheatgrass.* If we eat three times a day, we should "eliminate" three times a day. I realize that this is not only rare for women but much more difficult during pregnancy. The problem with this condition is that unreleased stool will be reabsorbed into our bodies. This can't be good for our babies. A great natural solution is wheatgrass juice. I could write an entire chapter on the benefits of this incredible elixir.

Those who share my enthusiasm for wheatgrass claim that one ounce of wheatgrass juice has the vitamins, minerals, and amino acids of two and a half pounds of green vegetables. They also tout numerous health benefits of wheatgrass and suggest that it not only improves digestion but also neutralizes toxins and carcinogens, helps blood sugar problems, prevents tooth decay, keeps hair from turning gray, and lowers high blood pressure.[1]

6. *Don't wallow in self-pity.* What you focus on will come to you, so focus on the positive aspects of pregnancy. It is easy to get caught up in the millions of little complaints that can arise as our bodies grow and nurture another human life. Don't listen to "negative Nellies." When I was a child, I associated anyone I disliked with Nellie Oleson, the witchy little naysayer on *Little House on the Prairie.* I fondly use that term for pregnancy naysayers as well. Be impenetrable to their misery.

7. *Give away your microwave.* Microwaves are not recommended for heating a baby's bottle. Although the bottle may feel cool on the outside, the liquid inside may be hot enough to burn the baby's mouth and throat. In addition, using the microwave to heat a bottle can cause harmful changes: infant formulas may lose some vitamins, and expressed breast milk may lose some of its protective properties.[2]

   I also want to mention dish and dishwasher detergents, most of which are filled with toxic chemicals. We place our foods on plates that have been washed in chemical solutions and expect no harm to come to us. Is this logical?

8. *Give your baby the beat.* Playing music, especially in the third trimester, is a wonderful way to soothe, excite, and educate your soon-to-be genius. Select appropriate music, and buy headphones that lie flat on your stomach. I have purchased at

least thirty "infant music" CDs—from jazz lullabies to classi-
cal symphonies. My top recommendation is *Baby Neptune* by
Baby Einstein, which features music by Handel, Telemann,
Beethoven, and Strauss.

9. *Create a baby affirmation.* Affirmations are a way to replace negative thoughts with positive ones in our conscious and subconscious mind. Honest mothers will admit that they sometimes
think about horror stories that could happen to their new and
unborn babies. Saying a daily affirmation not only creates positive energy and bonding with your unborn child but also
allows you to focus on your intentions for this new life. For
example, "My baby will be healthy, wealthy, and wise. He will
be smart, generous, and kind and possess all the traits required
to be the leader of the free world."

10. *Take professional pregnancy photos.* The key word is "professional." We are sensitive enough about our bodies during pregnancy that spending the few extra dollars on professional
photos is an investment well made. I admit that I had much
resistance to this idea, thinking I would certainly remember
ballooning to the size of Jabba the Hutt without photos to
record the event. However, the photos completely changed my
perception of my larger-than-life appearance. Don't get carried
away. One to three outfit changes is sufficient. These are memories you will regret not capturing.

11. *Select your pediatrician before you give birth.* In fact, most pediatricians will be more likely to make room for you in their
already-filled schedules if they know they are treating a baby
from birth forward. This may sound odd, but many frustrated
women confirmed this statement repeatedly: "The best time to
find a doctor for your baby is when your baby hasn't yet
arrived."

12. *Avoid heartburn medication.* The best advice I received from very smart women and many nurses was to avoid heartburn medication if at all possible. If you feel you have to have it, be sure to combine an ample amount of liquid with your dose of antacid; otherwise, you may develop kidney stones following birth.

    Kidney stones can be caused by hypercalciuria, a condition that occurs when there is too much calcium in the urine. According to the Alternative-Medicine-and-Health Web site, "You may be ingesting too much calcium, either through supplements (for example, Tums or other antacids), or through stomach acid medications, or even your drinking water. . . Reduce your calcium intake to the minimum required amount, which is about 600 to 1,000 mg. daily."[3]

13. *Splurge on your own breast pump.* Don't accept a friend's offer to lend you her breast pump. Be gracious and appreciative of the offer, but gently decline. I was advised that harmful bacteria can be stored in breast pumps even after they have been sterilized with boiling water. All breast pump manufacturers recommend a thorough cleaning every day. But since many women might not have the time or willingness to complete such a cleaning, it's better to be safe than sorry.

14. *Choose your rocking chairs carefully.* Consider your height when selecting a glider/rocking chair for you and your new baby. I made the mistake of spending $700 on a very sophisticated glider that gave me foot cramps. Your feet must comfortably touch the ground, or the annoyance will obliterate the benefit.

15. *Indulge in massages.* It is important to receive massages at any time in your life but especially when you are pregnant. Be sure to hire a qualified pregnancy masseuse so that no birthing pressure points are triggered. Also learn how to give infant

massages to your baby as an additional way to bond and relieve his or her stress and woes.

16. *Install the infant car seat early.* I have been told many stories about the agitating experience of first-time parents leaving the hospital: Dad swears and fumbles around in the backseat of the car, Mom stands in the hospital parking lot with their new-born, and both try to figure out the car seat instructions. Install your car seat before you go to the hospital, well before your due date, just to be safe.

17. *Pack your hospital bag early.* Your hospital bag should be ready to go up to six weeks in advance of your due date if you're a "planner" and at least one week in advance if you're a "procras-tinator." Make sure to include your favorite sanitary napkins, "granny panties," and a change of clothes for the baby, includ-ing a hat.

18. *Learn CPR.* God willing, you will never have to perform CPR on your infant, but knowledge is power. The peace of mind that a four-hour class provides is well worth the time and min-imal expense.

19. *Overinvite to your shower.* The number of people invited to your baby shower is much more critical than the number of people invited to your bridal shower. When we marry, we have spe-cific ideas about what we want and need. Many gifts that we receive are helpful but not essential. When we are about to give birth for the first time, we have no idea how much "stuff" we will need on a daily basis, so more is better. I can't tell you the extreme relief I experienced when I left my baby shower with almost every item on my registry.

20. *"Milk" it.* Everyone loves a pregnant woman. Make the most of it while you can because, thank goodness, it's temporary. No one will question, judge, or even hold a grudge because of your

odd, unpredictable, or flaky behavior. The "pregnancy card" trumps all other excuses.

Bonus tip: *Bank the cord blood.* Make a unique investment in your family's health. According to the Cord Blood Registry, "Cord blood, also known as 'placental blood,' is the blood that remains in the umbilical cord and placenta following birth and after the cord is cut. It's . . . a rich source of stem cells. Many families are now choosing to bank these genetically unique cord blood stem cells for the future health of their loved ones."[4]

Where to Give Back

Throughout this book I have stressed the idea that putting your-self first is the *least selfish* thing you can do for others because it gives you more to give back. I hope by now you agree with me. If you need ideas for places where you can give back, this list can be a starting point. All of these organizations are doing important work, and all of them would appreciate your help.

The Alliance for Children's Rights
http://www.kids-alliance.org
Since 1992 the Alliance for Children's Rights has helped more than fifty thousand children in Los Angeles County: children living in foster care, children with learning disabilities, children who need medical treatment or public benefits, and children who need legal guardians or adoption. The alliance offers legal services, community education, and advocacy, and it works to protect the rights and future of children for generations to come.

American Association of University Women
http://www.aauw.org
Since 1881 the American Association of University Women has been promoting education and equity for women and girls. The AAUW

has more than one hundred thousand members in thirteen hundred branches in the United States, Guam, and Puerto Rico. You can probably find one near you. The AAUW Educational Foundation is the world's largest source of funding exclusively for graduate women.

American Breast Cancer Foundation
http://www.abcf.org
The American Breast Cancer Foundation works to provide early detection education and screening services to those in need, no matter what age, race, sex, or financial challenge. The foundation also assists patients and their families and supports research for a cure.

Amnesty International USA
http://www.amnestyusa.org
Amnesty International USA is the U.S. branch of Amnesty International, a Nobel Prize–winning grass-roots activist organization with over 1.8 million members worldwide. Founded in 1961, Amnesty International undertakes research and action to prevent and end grave abuses of the rights to physical and mental integrity, freedom of conscience and expression, and freedom from discrimination, and it works to promote all human rights.

Food for Life Vrindavan
http://www.fflvrindavan.org
For the past ten years this humanitarian association has worked in the poorest villages in the Vrindavan area (near New Delhi, India). The association distributes food and clothing, offers basic medical assistance, and provides training for women, assistance to the elderly and disabled, and primary education for disadvantaged children.

Girl Talk

http://www.desiretoinspire.org

Girl Talk is a student-to-student mentoring program that pairs middle school girls with high school girls who listen and offer support and guidance when needed. The program helps middle school girls build self-esteem and gives high school girls a sense of accomplishment. Founded in 2002 and based in Atlanta, Georgia, Girl Talk has chapters in twenty-one states, reaching over ten thousand girls.

GlobalGiving

http://www.globalgiving.com

Founded by two former World Bank executives, GlobalGiving used the Internet to create a highly efficient marketplace. Donors can browse through projects by geography or by themes such as healthcare, environment, and education. Because GlobalGiving enables donors to give directly to projects, they know exactly where their money is going. Donors can see progress updates on most projects as funding is received and goals are met.

International Women's Health Coalition

http://www.iwhc.org

The International Women's Health Coalition promotes and protects the rights of women and girls worldwide. The coalition envisions a world where women are free from discrimination, sexual coercion, and violence; where they make free and informed choices on sexuality and reproduction; and where health information and services are accessible to all.

Madre

http://www.madre.org

Madre is a human rights organization that does much more than document and condemn abuses. The organization works with women who are affected by human rights violations to help them win justice and, ultimately, change the conditions that give rise to abuses. The group also challenges U.S. policies that undermine human rights. Over the years, it has developed an internationally recognized model of human rights in action.

National Domestic Violence Hotline
http://www.ndvh.org
Established as part of the Violence Against Women Act passed by Congress in 1996, the National Domestic Violence Hotline is available to callers 24 hours a day, 365 days a year. It responds to more than sixteen thousand calls each month. If you or someone you know is frightened about something in your relationship, please call the National Domestic Violence Hotline at (800) 799-SAFE (7233) or TTY (800) 787-3224. For its tenth anniversary the hotline has organized the Decade for Change Summit to outline a ten-year initiative to reduce domestic violence by 2016.

Introduction

1. *American Heritage Dictionary of the English Language*, 4th ed., s.v. "martyr," Answers.com, http://www.answers.com/topic/martyr.
2. Pat Robertson, quoted in John Bill, "Pat Robertson's Other Not-So-Famous Quotes, *Blogcritics*, August 25, 2005, http://blogcritics .org/archives/2005/08/25/024237.php.

Principle One

1. See, for example, Zannah Hackett, *The Ancient Wisdom of Matchmaking: The Knowledge of Y.O.U.* (Lincoln, NE: iUniverse, 2005). Others who discuss these laws include Brian Tracy (http://www .BrianTracy.com/) and Robert E. Drier (http://www.crcsite.org/karma.htm).
2. Stormynightout, posting on Jokes and Tall Tales, eBay Forums, October 5, 2005, http://forums.ebay.com/db1/thread.jspa ?thread ID=1000089691&start=40.
3. Thomas Willhite, *Living Synergistically* (Clearlake Oaks, CA: PSI World, 1975).

Principle Two

1. Louann Brizendine, *The Female Brain* (New York: Morgan Road Books, 2006).
2. Ibid., book jacket.

3. Amitai Etzioni, quoted in Daniel Goleman, *Emotional Intelligence* (New York: Bantam Books, 1995), 285.

Principle Three

1. Josh and Amanda, "Real Newspaper Ads," JoshAndAmanda Blog, August 1, 2006, http://blog.joshandamanda.com/.
2. Hewitt Associates, "Hewitt Study Highlights Squeeze on Retirement Savings," BNET, November 2005, http://job functions.bnet.com.
3. Oprah Winfrey, "This Is the Year to Get Richer," *The Oprah Winfrey Show*, ABC, January 22, 2007, http://www.oprah .com/money/jeanchatzky/slides/20070122/jeanchatzky _stories _350_103.jhtml.
4. *Dictionary.com Unabridged*, ver. 1.1, s.v. "couple," Dictionary .com, http://dictionary.reference.com/browse/couple.
5. Deborah Siegel, "The New Trophy Wife," *Psychology Today*, January/February 2004.
6. Ibid.
7. Nando Pelusi, quoted ibid.
8. Frank Pittman, quoted ibid.
9. "Who Wears the Pants?" Stupid Jokes, *MIStupid,com*, May 9, 2002, http://www.mistupid.com/jokes/page025.htm.
10. Outskirts, "Celibacy," ilovebacon.com, November 11, 2003, http://www.ilovebacon.com/111103/k.shtml.
11. Mary Cavaliere, quoted in Susan Orenstein, "100 Years of Attitude," *Real Simple*, May 2006.
12. Hebrew Talmud, quoted by Dawn Maracle, "About Women," DawnMaracle.com, http://www.dawnmaracle.com/id28.htm.
13. "The Wedding Test," Holties House Blog, January 9, 2007, http://holtieshouse.blogspot.com/search?q=wedding+test.

14. Ken Barnes, *Ten Things Women Do to Screw Up a Man's Life* (Bloomington, IN: 1st Books Library, 2003), 63.
15. Ibid., 64.
16. The 'Naut, "Dear Diary: Hers vs. His," Monkeynaut Blog, May 19, 2005, http://monkeynaut.blogspot.com.

Principle Four

1. Laura Desmond, quoted in "View from the Top," *Wall Street Journal Online,* November 20, 2006, http://online.wsj.com/public/article/SB116377878729526354.html?mod=2_1258_.
2. Ursula M. Burns, quoted in "View from the Top."
3. Brizendine, *The Female Brain,* 37.
4. Ibid.
5. Hacsi Horvath, "Heart Attack More Likely to Kill Women Than Men," CNN.com, July 26, 1999, http://www.rdono.com/ health/heart/9907/21/gender.heart/index.html.
6. Julie Buring and Nancy Ferrari, "Take an Aspirin and . . .," *Newsweek,* April 24, 2006, 71.
7. "Valentine's Day RX for Single Women over 50," eNotAlone, http://www.enotalone.com/article/3800.html.
8. Spider, "I Have the Breasts of an 18-Year-Old," Old Folks Jokes, PNJ.com, January 21, 2007, www.forums.pnj.com/viewtopic.php?=&p=59293.
9. Frank Kaiser, "In Praise of Older Women," *Suddenly Senior,* 2000, http://www.suddenlysenior.com/praiseolderwomen.html.

Principle Five

1. Christopher, "Friendship & the Difference," Chris vs Chris, March 29, 2007, www.chrisvschris.com/friendship-the -difference/.

2. Don't Know What to Make of This, "Mom Job Description," November 30, 2006, http://selfmademom.net/2006/11/.
3. "A Princess in Distress," *People*, February 27, 2006, 135.
4. Nancy Peretsman, quoted in "View from the Top."
5. L. H. Sanders, "Eleven Tips on Getting More Efficiency Out of Women Employees," *Mass Transportation*, July 1943, Success Performance Solutions, http://www.super-solutions .com/1943 GuidetoHiringWomen.asp.
6. Brizendine, *The Female Brain*, 22.
7. Joan C. Williams, Jessica Manvell, and Stephanie Bornstein, *"Opt Out" or Pushed Out? How the Press Covers Work/Family Conflict* (San Francisco: The Center for WorkLife Law, University of California, Hastings College of the Law, 2006).
8. "Women and the World Economy: A Guide to Womenomics," *The Economist*, April 12, 2006, cited in Williams, Manvell, and Bornstein, *"Opt Out" or Pushed Out?*
9. S. M. Bianchi, "Maternal Employment and Time with Children: Dramatic Change or Surprising Continuity," *Demography* 37, no. 4 (2000).
10. Joshua Holland, "Womenomics 101," *Pasadena Weekly*, July 6, 2006.
11. Carol Bartz, quoted in "View from the Top."

Epilogue

1. SJ, comment on "Empowered Woman: Pussycat Doll or Call Girl?" Saundra Pelletier Blog, comment posted March 25, 2007, http://www.saundrapelletier.com/blog_detail/19_ Empowered _Woman_Pussycat_Doll_or_Call_Girl.

Appendix B

1. Ask Yahoo! "What Are the Nutritional Benefits of Wheatgrass Juice?" http://ask.yahoo.com/20010802.html.

2. Anthony Wayne and Lawrence Newell, "Radiation Ovens: The Proven Dangers of Microwaves," CureZone.com, http://www .curezone.com/foods/microwave_oven_risk.asp.

3. Alternative-Medicine-and-Health, LLC, "Kidney Stones," http://ashmd.com/conditions/kidney.htm.

4. Cord Blood Registry, http://www.cordblood.com/im/gift /feeder /stemcellnews.asp?id=easy.

acting like a woman, 129–131
advice, seeking, 36–37
advocacy, self-, 127
affirmations, 166
Albright, Madeleine, 20
allies/alliances, 83–84, 133–134
anxiety, 28
athletes, 19
attitude, 118, 141–148
attraction between men and women, 60

baby showers, 168
backstabbers, 134
balance, 4, 80, 139
Barnes, Ken, 75
bartering services, 84
Bartz, Carol, 139
bonding, 87
boundaries, in relationships, 80
bravado, 122
breast-feeding, 87
breast pumps, 167
Brizendine, Louanne, 47, 135
bullies, 133–134
Burns, Ursula M., 85–86

calcium, 167
Cavaliere, Mary, 70
cavalries
    concept of, 7, 79–81
    emotional pillars, 84–89
    hiring your, 90–94
    members of, 83–90
    strategic allies, 83–84
    taskmasters, 89–90
celebrities, 19–21
change(s), 14, 34, 62
character, 51

choices, 42–43, 144
cognitive behavioral therapy, 142–143
communication
    making needs/desires known, 54
    negotiation skills, 115–116
    in office politics, 135
    responsibility for good, 37–38
Compensation, Law of, 23
competence, 132
competitive feminism, 103–112.
    See also feminists/feminism
complacency, 18
compromise, 31–32
confidence, 45, 120–126
conflict resolution, 116
confrontation management, 115–116
constipation, 164
Cord Blood Registry, 169
core values
    alignment with, 4, 15, 44
    clarifying your, 7, 28–29
    of deliberate creators, 21
    identifying your, 43–44
    multitasking and, 42
Correspondence, Law of, 23
couples/partnerships, 57–58. See
    also relationships; relationships
    with men
Couric, Katie, 19
CPR, 168
credit for your success, 126–129

daughter-mother relationships,
    84–87
decision making, martyr mentality
    and, 2–3
decisiveness, 29
delegation, 128–129

deliberate creators
  actions of, 28–35
  deciding to be, 6–7
  description of, 11–12
  examples of, 19–21
  feminism and, 5
  focus of, 142
  how to become, 26–27
  outlook of, 139
  qualities of, 27–28
  truths known by, 35–38
denial, 34, 74, 145–147
Desmond, Laura, 82
devil's advocacy, 124
diplomacy, 52
divorce, 58–59
dreams, compromising your, 5

emotional intelligence, 51–52
emotional needs, 148
emotional pillars, 84–89
emotions
  control over, 21
  negotiation and, 115–116
  women's versus men's, 47
empowerment, 109
enchanting waltz style, 100–102
ends justifying the means, 30
enemies, managing, 133–134
escapism, 147
estradiol, 98
Etzioni, Amitai, 51
exercise, 45–46
expectations in relationships, 80
extremism, 147–148

feedback, 131–132
The Female Brain (Brizendine), 47
feminists/feminism, 4–5, 70,
  103–112
fidelity, 70–78
fiery tango style, 98–100
finances, 56–59
flatliners, 14–18, 21, 80, 139, 145
flexibility, 137–139
focusing on your wants, 26–27

forgiveness versus permission,
  127–128
friendship, men's versus women's,
  107

gifts, women's
  intuition, 46–52
  multitasking, 41–46
goals, SMART, 114, 147
Gumbel, Bryant, 19

hair care, 164
healthcare providers, 97
heart attacks, 94–95
heartburn, 167
help, seeking/accepting, 37
heroes, 61–66, 77
Hewitt Associates, 56
hobbies, 45–46

incompetence, 132
infant car seats, 168
infidelity, 70–78
inflexibility, 138
information, dealing with lack of,
  124–125
inner growth, 149
insecurity, 122
insight, 52
instincts, 46–47
integrity, 29, 54
intentional living, 142, 144
intuition, 4, 46–52, 112

Kaiser, Frank, 100–101
kidney stones, 167
King, Billie Jean (Billie Jean Moffitt),
  19

laws of nature, 21–26
leadership qualities, 122, 132, 137
Love, Law of, 24, 53–54
loyalty, 57–58, 107–108, 131–132

male-female compatibility, 55
mantras, 149

martyr mentality, 1–3, 4, 40, 145
Masako, Princess, 111
massages, 167–168
meaning, 35–36, 118, 148
memories, 43
men, relationships with
    attraction between men
        and women, 60
    expectations/boundaries in, 80
    infidelity, 70–78
    male-female compatibility, 55
    mothering husbands, 66–70
    sex, 74–78
    taking the lead, 7, 53
    trophy wives, 59–61
    in work settings, 62–63
menopause, 95–98
microwaves, 165
Mischell, Dan, 98
mission statements, 28–29, 44–45
Mommy Wars, 104–112
money management, 56–59
morning sickness, 163–164
mother-daughter relationships,
    84–87
motherhood, 104–112
mothering husbands, 66–70
mothering tendencies, 125–126
mothers-in-law, 87–89
mother-son relationships, 87–89
multitasking, 41–46
music, 165–166

nature, universal laws of, 21–26
naysayers, 124
negotiations, 115–116, 135
nonresistant attitude, 141

obstacles, sensing hidden, 52
office politics, 135
opinions of others, 117–118
optimism, 21
Orenstein, Susan, 70
organization, 124
Orman, Suze, 19–20
oxytocin, 87

parenting, as job, 109–111
paying it forward, 27, 101
pediatricians, 166
Pelusi, Nandi, 59–60
Peretsman, Nancy, 117
permission versus forgiveness,
    127–128
personal assistants, 90–94
persuasion, 135
photography, 166
physical appearance, 145–146,
    164
Pittman, Frank, 60
placental blood, 169
politics, office, 135
possessions, 124
possibility thinking, 21, 26
power of intention, 144
pregnancy tips, 163–169
prenatal care, 163
preparation, 123–124
presentations, tips for giving,
    123–124
principles for achievement, 6–7
priorities/prioritization, 42
prosperity, 37

Queen Bee Syndrome, 112–113

relationships
    building political, 135
    mother-daughter, 84–87
    with mothers-in-law, 87–89
    mother-son, 87–89
    office politics, 135
    treating everyone as equals,
        135–137
    unfulfilling, 54
    with women, 81–83, 103–104,
        112–113 (*See also* cavalries;
        competitive feminism)
relationships with men
    attraction between men and
        women, 60
    expectations/boundaries in, 80
    infidelity, 70–78

relationships with men, *continued*
  male-female compatibility, 55
  mothering husbands, 66–70
  sex, 74–78
  taking the lead, 7, 53
  trophy wives, 59–61
  in work settings, 62–63
resistance, 141
resources
  books, 151–156
  Web sites, 156–161, 171–174
respect, 36–37, 108
responsibility, for happiness, 55
rightsizing, 124
risk taking, 118, 126
rivals, 133–134
Robertson, Pat, 4

self-acceptance, 21
self-esteem, 45
self-exploration, 117, 118
self-pity, 12–13, 165
self-promotion, 127
self-reflection, 43
self-respect, 36, 57
self-worth account, 35
servitude, 40
sex, 74–78
Siegel, Deborah, 59
SMART goals, 114, 147
Speroff, Leon, 98
stem cells, 169
strategic allies, 83–84
stress reduction, 94–95
stretch marks, 164
success
  barriers to, 121
  comfort with, 7, 129–139
  obstacles to, 120
  sacrifices for, 27
  setting others up for, 65–66
  setting SMART goals for, 114, 147
  three Cs of, 117–129

support systems, 99. *See also*
  cavalries
Surrender, Law of, 23–24

taking the lead, 53
Talmud, 70
taskmasters, 89–90
television personalities, 19–20
*Ten Things Women Do to Screw Up
  a Man's Life* (Barnes), 75
Test and Treat program, 97–98
Three, Law of, 22, 74
three Cs of success. *See also* success
  confidence, 120–126
  overview of, 117–121
  taking credit, 126–129
  treatment of others, 135–137
trophy wives, 59–61
trust building, 131–132
trust in yourself, 36
Turner, Tina, 20

unfulfilling relationships, 54
universal laws of nature, 21–26

victims, 12–14, 21, 139

wake-up calls, 145–146
Waring, Marilyn, 138–139
Web sites, 156–161, 167
wheatgrass juice, 164–165
Willhite, Thomas, 26
Winfrey, Oprah, 57
women, relationships with, 81–83,
  103–104, 112–113. *See also*
  cavalries; competitive feminism
Word, Law of the, 22–23
work settings, relationships in,
  62–63, 135
World War II workforce guidelines,
  120

THE AUTHOR

S aundra Pelletier is a writer, seminar leader, and Empower-Mentor, as well as a life coach and an expert on women's healthcare from puberty to menopause. She successfully maneuvered her way from picking potatoes in Caribou, Maine, to living her passion—helping women get the results they desire both personally and professionally. Known for her dynamic leadership, she became a successful business executive by playing and winning the corporate game. She has fourteen years' experience in the pharmaceutical industry, where she rapidly rose to leadership positions and successfully launched pharmaceutical brands all over the world.

At Searle Laboratories, Saundra served as global new business director and leader for international franchises and accounted for $250 million in revenue. She nearly tripled sales as vice president of pharmaceuticals for Women First HealthCare, a NASDAQ-listed specialty pharmaceutical company. In addition, she has conducted significant quantitative and qualitative market research on women's issues.

Saundra earned her bachelor of science degree in business, with a concentration in marketing, from Husson College in Bangor, Maine, where in 2001 she became the youngest inductee into the Husson College Hall of Fame. She also holds an associate degree in business communication from the New England School of Broadcasting in Bangor. She is certified as a life and career coach by the Life Purpose Institute in San Diego, California, as well as a Level III Y.O.U. Practitioner. For the past ten years she has helped numerous clients live their lives in a deliberate and purposeful way.

She is a member of Team Women, the San Diego Professional Coaches Alliance, Women's Global Network, the National Organization for Women, National Association of Women Business Owners, and Business Mastery Network.

Saundra lives with her husband and son in Encinitas, California.

Saundra Pelletier
EmpowerMentor
Providing Guidance and Clarity
WWW.SAUNDRAPELLETIER.COM

Saundra's passion is and always has been working with people to get their best results both personally and professionally. Her personal mantra is "never confuse motion with action," and she is committed to helping her clients not only achieve results but exceed expectations.

KEYNOTE SPEECHES

Saundra is a highly skilled speaker whose presentations have been called inspiring, powerful, enlightening, informative, life-changing, and fun. Presentation topics include the following:

- Professional Leadership: EQ vs. IQ
- The Battle of Balance: How to Get More Out of Life
- Victim, Flatliner, or Deliberate Creator: How to Get More of What You Want
- Mastering a Deliberate Mind-Set to Achieve Results
- Rocks and Water: How the Opposite Sexes Can Better Coexist Personally and Professionally

Some of the groups that have been inspired by Saundra:

DirectSelling Women's Alliance
eWomen Network
The Executive Women's Council
Rancho Santa Fe Women in Business Group
San Diego Professional Coaches Alliance
San Diego Women Inc.
Southern California CPAs
Scripps Hospital
Team Women
Women's Global Network

All-day seminars are available for men and women throughout the year.

Putting Yourself First: Level One—
Never Confuse Motion with Action

- The differences between a victim, a flatliner, and a deliberate creator
- Steps required to become a deliberate creator and maximize your results
- How to impact people with different personality types to improve relationships
- The importance of core values and how to determine what those values are
- Why our attitude determines our prosperity in every aspect of our lives

Putting Yourself First: Level Two—
Seek the Truth and Agree with It

- The total knowledge of Y.O.U.
- A better understanding of yourself and what motivates you
- Significantly transform all your relationships
- The seven attitudes that ensure success
- The three types of cavalry members that can help you get results

Saundra specializes in empowering people to see their strengths, improving relationships, stimulating career growth and creating a healthy lifestyle. Her coaching style is straightforward, lighthearted, honest and compassionate. She will challenge you to find your own answers—supporting you each step along the way and helping you to live a successful and happy life as defined by you.

Continuing professional education credits are available to healthcare and wellness professionals for all seminars. Continuing professional education credits are provided through collaboration with Patti Biro and Associates, Professional Education Consultants.

- Dentists
- Dental hygienists
- Dental assistants
- Licensed professional counselors
- Massage therapists
- Registered nurses
- Social workers

SAUNDRA PELLETIER

Saundra Pelletier International

2033 San Elijo Avenue, #222

Cardiff, CA 92004

Phone: **(858) 354-6378**

E-mail: **info@saundrapelletier.com**